THE STUDENT, NEWS WATCHER AND COUCH POTATO GUIDE TO THE U.S. CONSTITUTION

Pete Bohaczyk

To a friend of a friend,
I hope that you enjoy
the book!
Pete Bohaczyk

UNIVERSITY PRESS OF AMERICA

Lanham • New York • London

University Press of America®, Inc.
4720 Boston Way
Lanham, Maryland 20706

3 Henrietta Street
London WC2E 8LU England

Printed in the United States of America
British Cataloging in Publication Information Available

Library of Congress Cataloging-in-Publication Data

Bohaczyk, Pete.
The student, news watcher, and couch potato guide to the U.S. Constitution / Pete Bohaczyk.
p. cm.
1. United States—Constitutional law—Popular works. I. Title.
KF4550.Z9B64 1991
342.73'02—dc20 [347.3022] 91-17708 CIP

ISBN 0–8191–8313–X (pbk. : alk. paper)

The paper used in this publication meets the minimum requirements of American National Standard for Information Sciences—Permanence of Paper for Printed Library Materials, ANSI Z39.48–1984.

To my wife, Sue
who gives me encouragement
when I need it.

I would like to acknowledge Mrs. Mary Heady, the mother of a good friend, who so graciously used her time to read my manuscript. As a college student I took my English term papers to her for grammatical scrutiny and correction. Many years later she found herself once again, "undangling" my participles.

I would also like to acknowledge Chuck Copeland, CEO of CATS Magazine for his computer expertise and the borrowed use of the magazine facilities for the preparation of my manuscript.

TABLE OF CONTENTS

INTRODUCTION

When I first informed my classes each year that we were to begin a study of the United States Constitution, with few exceptions I could anticipate the reaction that was in store for me. I could see it coming; the wrinkled up noses and the grunts and groans, the shuffling in their seats and the ever present teenage remark, "BORING!!" It was very gratifying to know that after a few days there was a shifting of attitudes on the part of my students. Some began to really show an interest in this document, especially when we got to the Amendments. Amazingly, some of my worse discipline problems became very interested and would freely give first hand information about their own confrontations with the law and how the amendments were used on their behalf. For many years, what was a three week unit on the Constitution turned out to be a six week marathon, simply because the curiosity was there.

To many Americans the Constitution is a much revered but rather boring document. Many swear to uphold and protect it, others protest - sometimes violently in its behalf, and some even die for it in times of war, however, few will take the time to look over its contents. Most of what it says remains hidden from view except for those few emotion arousing provisions that are constantly in the public awareness - such as the First, Second, Fifth and Sixth Amendments.

Those who have been through school have been exposed to this document but, like everything else, neglect enters the picture. We seem to neglect that which we do not use and we forget that which is neglected. This is human nature, I am sure. There are many things that I have forgotten in science and mathematics, simply because I do not use them and they slip down to the lower rungs on my ladder of priorities.

I imagine that our knowledge of the Constitution would slip down farther on our priority ladder if it were not for the fact that reference to some of it is constantly made in the newspaper and on television. "I plead the fifth amendment," became a household word and an expression that people of all ages used because of its constant media exposure during the numerous Senate hearings that had begun in the 1950's. How often has reference been made to the first amendment's freedom of speech and the second amendment's right to bear arms? Who can add to the fight between the advocates of capital punishment and those who feel that this is a violation of the eighth amendment's cruel or unreasonable punishment?

The purpose of this book is to enable the reader to have a little better understanding of the United States Constitution; what the document consists of and how and why certain provisions were incorporated. Hopefully, as a result, there will be more insight and understanding on the part of the reader whenever references to the Constitution are made on television, in the newspapers and in general conversation.

This is not a scholarly book. It does not dissect, analyze or search for hidden meanings. It is not for the student of government to use in his pursuit of higher degrees, nor is it for the student of jurisprudence. It will be a simple "refresher course" for those interested souls who follow the currents of conflict and change in our society and would like to know just a little more about our Constitution than they already know. It can be used as a supplemental source for those about to embark on the study of government or on Constitution. Last but not least it is for the couch potato who is bombarded by his television set with references to the Constitution and the Amendments, as he watches detective stories, talk shows and the nightly news.

As a student I was interested in the cause and effect of things. As a teacher I relied heavily on making my students aware of the reasons that brought about changes. In this manner this book is set up. I will try to incorporate, as much as possible, the idea of how government has developed, why the constitution came into existence, the reasons for the provisions within the Constitution and I will also attempt to bring to life the various clauses by utilizing anecdotes whenever possible.

Hopefully, this book will explain the many provisions within the Constitution that were placed there because of a reaction to unfavorable experiences suffered in the life drama of the colonies and later the young nation. The reason for the creation of the Constitution itself will be an important part of this cause and effect application. A fair amount of American History can be learned simply by studying the Constitution and the amendments and the forces that brought them about.

I realize I must develop the same interest for my readers as had to be developed for my students or this book will not be successful. It should be realized, however, that sometimes points must be made that are not as exciting as others may be. This is true in almost every endeavor. Some things are naturally more exciting or interesting, or some things are more interesting to one person than to another. This is the way of the world.

I taught the United States Constitution as part of my history course to the toughest audience in the world - eighth graders. In order to keep their attention on focus, situations and stories had to be incorporated to parallel and give enhancement to what they believed to be - in their popular parlance, "boring!" Success seemed to be achieved to some degree because for eight years I taught large groups of sometimes between 100 and 160 students in one class. When it was all over I had taught the Constitution and American History for twenty seven of my thirty years as a teacher and I will not even venture a guess as to the number of students that sat in my classrooms in the many years that I spent in the "trenches."

CHAPTER 1 WHERE DID IT ALL BEGIN?

There are many philosophical approaches to explaining the reason for the development of government. Let us use two basic ideas and say that many concepts of government can be broken down into these two basic types.

One concept contends that government was formed to benefit man. John Locke, a 17th century English philosopher, stated that governments were formed to protect life, liberty and property. This sounds vaguely familiar doesn't it? Jefferson was a great reader of John Locke and was influenced by him when he wrote our Declaration of Independence.

Let's take a trip in our time machine and go back to the very beginning of man living his life in caves. In order to hunt some of the game for food, cooperation was needed because they were "not talking rabbits." In fact it was up for grabs as to who was finally the hunter and who the hunted. Leadership usually fell into the hands of the strongest and most cunning hunter who was looked up to with great respect. Cave men also banded together to protect themselves from the neighboring tribe that came and pillaged upon them. They soon learned that the more cooperation that was practiced among the group, the more protection they could have and the more they could get accomplished. Thus was developed the idea that governments were formed for the protection and enhancement of the individual.

We do not really know whether it happened this way or not, but it makes for an interesting story. There will be mention to this paragraph again when we review the Declaration of Independence.

On the other side of the coin we have the concepts brought forth by some of the other philosophers, such as Georg Hegel, that the government was the most important thing and man's purpose was to serve that government. Sometimes the premise that man was basically bad came into play here and that was the reason for governments being in total control.

In fact many of the books that were thrown on the bonfires during the infamous book burnings that took place upon the ascent of Hitler into power in the 1930's, were books that were geared to the first of the two mentioned philosophies.

Whether government started for the first reason or the second reason is academic because most governments in history, over a period of time, became oppressive. It seems that the leaders of government were selected from those who were strong and cunning enough to hunt food and to protect the tribe or nation. Human nature being as it is, one can imagine the results of the most physical, smartest, most cunning, and daring, being in complete control. To ensure his control, the leader would gather around him those possessed of the same qualities that he had - to a lesser extent of course. The procedure was to eliminate anyone who had the same qualities that the leader possessed, because these attributes became a threat to the man in charge. The eventual destiny of the weaker and poorer were to serve those who were in power. Sometimes the government was considerate to its people because of a good and just ruler; however, most of the time it was bad. There are many cases in history where a good and just ruler was followed by a very tyrannical son. Whether bad or good, the people within a government had little choice, as a dog has little choice as to whether or not he winds up with a good or bad master.

It is realized that this is a very elementary method of explaining a very complex concept of government but for our purpose, it is adequate. One can see this simple explanation of government in the War Lords and Emperors of China and in the Emperors and the Samurai of Japan. It was very much evident in the Knights and Kings of Feudal Europe in the middle ages.

A philosopher of government named Machiavelli wrote in 1532 that a ruler should be concerned with only power and does not have to live up to any ethical standards that others must follow. His works have been a rationalization for the despotism and tyranny practiced by many European rulers.

It was an added assurance to his maintenance of power if a ruler could impress upon his subjects that he had some sort of divine commission in his role as leader or that he was a god himself. Some governments developed a priestly class for the purpose of making sure that the people were kept under control through superstition and fear of the supernatural.

Many emperors had themselves deified (made into gods) as did the Roman and Japanese Emperors to name just two. In the middle ages the kings of Europe ruled by Divine Right. The Divine Righters could always prove their point by saying, "He rules, doesn't he? Therefore God wants him to rule." It is difficult to argue this point.

There was a light at the end of this tunnel of tyranny which will be seen when we review the incident that occurred at Runnymede, England in 1215.

THE INFLUENCE OF THE ENGLISH

Regardless of our heritage, most Americans are English in their way of thinking. Even though we are a "melting pot" of many cultures and nationalities, it had been the influence of English law and culture that had shaped our thoughts and patterned our institutions. The decisive proof of this is the fact that this book is being written in the English language and most American citizens could read and understand it if they wanted to. How English can one get?

For almost half of our existence we were thirteen British colonies. If we had to be owned by anybody, I believe that we were fortunate that we were owned by the British. During the 17th century, England was the most liberal country in the world. This situation allowed a certain amount of self rule to the English colonies.

Under the English government it was mostly individuals, united in business ventures (companies), that received charters from the English kings to set up colonies in the New World for the expressed purpose of profit. A king shared handsomely in these profits and this explained his willingness to give charters to these companies. He owned all that land but it wasn't turning a buck until it was put to good use. As long as the colonists met their contractual agreements to produce and send back food and raw materials to the companies for profit and as long as the colonists obeyed the laws of the king, they had the freedom to set up and control their own governments. The colonist learned very early how to govern themselves.

To find out how and why England became more liberal than the nations of Europe we must go back to a place called Runnymede in 1215. The kings of England were gaining too much power to suit the noble landowners so a group of these nobles got together and forced King John of England to sign a Charter limiting his power. This is considered the basis for English constitutional liberties. Of course this was an agreement between the land barons and the king and did not involve the common people, but later it was interpreted to mean all free men. In 1628 this document was reinforced by the Petition of Rights and in 1689 by the Bill of Rights, which had a great influence later, on our Bill of Rights. This document is known as the *Great Charter* or the *Magna Carta* or the *Magna Charta.*

THE RENAISSANCE

When barbarian hordes came down from Europe and gradually defeated the Roman Empire, Western Civilization went into a semi conscious state known as the Dark Ages. The conquerors were not as advanced culturally as the conquered. It was as though the lights went out in the area of advancement in most fields. There was a tiny light that remained lit in the monasteries where great works were being copied and placed on the shelves, to be saved for the time when a renewed interest in learning would once again be ignited.

It was as though Europe was in a deep sleep for over 1000 years. It slowly began to stir, yawn, stretch and awaken. This waking up period in Western History is referred to as the Renaissance. The order of the dark ages began to be shaken by men who painted, experimented and explored - sometimes under the fear of death. It was against this backdrop that Columbus accidentally discovered America while looking for a shorter trade route to the Indies. Evidence points to the fact that others came to our shores long before Columbus. Nothing was done about it, however, because the time was not right when they touched on our land. The world WAS ready to do something about it when Columbus made his discoveries.

Because of the Industrial Revolution, which was a direct result of the Renaissance, England and Western Europe began to assert themselves as the strongest nations in the world.

COLONIZATION

The Americas were explored and developed by Great Britain and the European countries because they got caught up in this Industrial Revolution and had an advantage over the rest of the world. They had the tools (technology of sailing, shipbuilding and weapons) to literally sail and make their influence felt throughout the world. To keep peace between Catholic Spain and Portugal, the Pope actually divided the earth in two and gave both Spain and Portugal half of it. England and several European countries began to question the ownership of the two halves of the earth by going out and obtaining colonies of their own. A few wars ensued to try to determine who was the "King of the Hill." Great effort in the form of sacrifice and expense were made by England and the Western Europeans to obtain colonies in the world. All this was for one purpose alone and that was exploitation of those new lands - pure and simple. The riches that they beheld in those land, had but one purpose - to be taken back to the mother country.

In the middle of the Eighteenth Century, Mother England still maintained this exploitative mentality which began to rub the American Colonists the wrong way. Some American colonists dreamed of independence and England still tried to tenaciously hold its exploitative grip on them. Something had to give.

CHAPTER 2 WE STARTED AS ENGLISHMEN

(The reader should be fully aware that there were other settlers from other countries that had a lot of influence in shaping the unique character of the American colonies. To keep this study from becoming too mired down I choose to elaborate on the English influence.)

In order to try to understand the change that took place in the attitudes of the English colonists as generation passed, let us develop a hypothetical settlement on a far away planet by a group of imaginary earth settlers and carry their society through several generations.

As the settlers "set sail" on their new venture I am sure that they were experiencing ambivalent emotions. They were suffering the pain of leaving their homes, loved ones and friends, possibly never to be seen again. On the other hand they were elated with the excitement of travel and development of a new home. Certainly they were going to take as much of the old world with them as they could. I'm sure they took books, films, video tapes, audio tapes and just about every reminder of earth that they were allowed to take on a space ship. More than likely they named their new settlement after the towns or states from which they came. They probably honored a president or governor by naming a settlement or a river after him or her. They put around them as many reminders of the "old earth" as they possibly could. What would be wrong with naming the planet onto which they build their new lives "New Earth" or "Earth II?"

As children were born, the first generation would begin to pass on, to their offspring, the stories and experiences that they had in their life on earth. Here was a situation whereby first hand experiences were passed on to a next generation whom never would experience these things first hand, because of the many light years of travel, and could never fully understand what it would be like to be an earthling. When the next generation came, the second generation would begin to tell the third generation second hand tales. As the generations passed, not only did these stories about earth tend to become more detached, distorted, forgotten and less interesting but a new force had been at work from the very first moment that the spaceship touched down on the new planet. The new land itself, with all its unique physical attributes, hardships and inconveniences, began to shape a new character in these settlers. This new environment began to change each generation, and just a few characteristics of the original settlers remained. New literature, music, concepts of law, architecture and speech came about and even though they still called themselves earthlings, they hardly resembled the original earth settlers. Those institutions that were brought from earth, that had continued to work for them, would probably still be kept, with modifications.

COLONIAL UNIQUENESS

We have here a parallel to the history of the American colonies. As generation after generation passed, there was a filtering process taking place. Englishmen first came and in the years previous to the Revolutionary War, we had Americans who called themselves Englishmen, but were more "American" in reality.

Not all were affected however, many were still so thoroughly English by the time of our War for Independence that they would not choose to fight against the British and actually helped or fought on the side of the English. These people were called Loyalists or Tories.

THE FRENCH AND INDIAN WAR

The biggest rift between the Americans and the mother country of England came after the French and Indian War which was fought in the mid 18th Century. Before this war, domination of North America was still up for grabs, especially between the French and English. It was a secure feeling on the part of the American colonists to have the power of the British Empire on their side. When the French began to move into the Ohio Valley to stake their claims, the Americans flocked to the side of the British. Colonel Washington, of the Virginia Militia and many others fought on the side of the British to remove the hated and feared French from their lands.

OUR ATTITUDE TOWARD ENGLAND CHANGED

American sentiment toward England began to change drastically after the fear of the French was removed. The very infamous problems that we have studied as students, those problems that precipitated our War for Independence, began to take place at this time.

Some of the reasons that caused this strife were: 1. England would not allow American settlers over the Appalachian Mountains. 2. England felt that Americans should help pay for the war (thus the taxes). 3. England had neglected the American colonies because of their many wars with France. Now that the threat of France had subsided, they began to enforce the laws that were already in existence but had been poorly enforced. This is similar to letting a child run wild for the first sixteen years of his life and all of a sudden the parents begin to try to discipline him. They might as well forget it. The colonists now began to look upon British troops not as protection but rather as a tool for enforcing British law. 4. We had leaders such as Sam Adams who would stop at nothing to achieve independence. They fanned the fires of revolution. Other reasons for the mounting tensions could be mentioned but this is enough to get a good message across.

It is very important in the study of the Constitution to understand, before we go any further, that a lot of what took place during this pre revolutionary period, left the framers of the constitution with a resolve that these "injustices," perpetrated upon the colonies by Great Britain, would not take place in the government that they were forming. They incorporated safeguards - clauses stated in such a way that these incidents would not be allowed to take place again. They also resolved to prevent the takeover of our government by individuals or groups. Keep this in mind because as these clauses are mentioned later, reference will be made to those particular events in history, and it will be brought to light the method by which our constitution is capable of checking those who desire to gain wrongful control.

I like to use the example of Washington Irving's, *Rip Van Winkle* story to bring home the idea of the drastic change that took place in the minds of some of the colonists toward the British. What is commonly known, Rip slept for twenty years, but what may not be realized is that he slept through some of the turbulent years of pre revolutionary American history and through the change of attitude toward the British that the colonists were experiencing. Upon waking he went back to his village and because of all the years that had gone by and because of his scraggly appearance - he wore a beard when beards were unfashionable - Rip was probably a sight to behold from the standpoint of the villagers. The inhabitants wanted to know who this unusual person was and how he voted - "whether he was a Federal or a Democrat." "Alas, gentleman," he (Rip) cried, somewhat dismayed, "I am a poor quiet man, a native of this place, and a loyal subject of the king, God Bless him!" Now THAT he never should have said - twenty years before it was a common expression but not in that revolutionary minded village. Immediately, one of the villagers yelled, "A Tory! A Tory! A spy!"

ENTER DOCUMENT NUMBER ONE

Relations began to deteriorate between England and her American colonies and by September 1774 the colonies decided that they should send delegates to a national assembly to determine whether a united effort for challenging these problems could be brought about. This was called the First Continental Congress. The colonies were in touch with one another for some time before this by an organization known as the Committee of Correspondence which sent messages from one colony to the next for the purpose of keeping abreast as to what was happening throughout the colonies. This committee seemed to be the seed that was planted which would flower into the United States of America much later. During the French and Indian War in a conference at Albany N.Y., an effort was made by Ben Franklin, to try to unite the colonies. It was turned down because the colonists at that time were not ready for such a radical venture.

This First Continental Congress met before the war started. They were not entirely together as to whether or not they should take drastic action and go for independence or to try to seek reconciliation with England. One important factor was their decision to have the states train their militia. Another important thing that they accomplished was their setting a time for the Second Continental Congress to be held. This meeting had taken place in Philadelphia because it was located about mid-point between the colonies. The location was important because of the time consuming and inconvenient mode of travel of the day, and because Philadelphia was at that time the largest city in the colonies.

The war began before the Second Continental Congress met. It was at this Congress that historic events took place. There was still division among the delegates as to the course of action to be taken. They sent a "Petition for a Redress of Grievances" to King George III of England, listing what they thought to be unjust actions on the part of England toward her colonies. They hoped that the mentioned grievances could be rectified. They also promised to be more law-abiding if rectification took place. The Olive Branch Petition, as it was called, was turned down by the king. George Washington was elected as Commander-in-Chief of the Continental Army. George had gained his reputation as a leader during the French and Indian War. A year later a committee was formed to prepare some sort of document to inform the world as to why the colonists were fighting the British.

It was completed on the 4th of July, 1776. (Yes, you guessed it, Independence Day!) John Adams felt that future generations would recognize this date, "with pomp and parade, with shows, games, sports, guns, bells, bonfires and illuminations from one end of this continent to the other."

THE DECLARATION OF INDEPENDENCE

When one sees a fight take place, the question that is automatically asked is, "Why are they fighting?" In many years as a teacher I had broken up more fights among students than I care to remember. One thing is certain, I have never heard a confession on the part of the pugilistic antagonists as to who was at fault. Governments and nations exhibit the same behavior. When conflict arises the people of all nations and the government of those nations involved want to know what the fighting is all about and who is at fault. To be considered the "good guys" in an armed conflict is very important in terms of enlisting support from the people at home, keeping other nations neutral, keeping nations from joining or aiding the other side and to either enlist aid and support or to have countries actually come in on your side as allies. Even Hitler tried to justify his first few territorial acquisitions until he knew for certain that the world had no desire to confront him and if they did, he was so sure of his might that it made no difference.

As was already stated, one task of the Second Continental Congress was to come up with a document which gave the world and the American Colonists an explanation for our armed stand against England. Thomas Jefferson and a few others were formed into a committee to accomplish this task. The result of the committee's endeavor was the Declaration of Independence. I am not going to copy this document because it is very available to anyone who would like to read it. I would like to write down a brief summary of it however and make reference to why certain points were made in this document.

The Declaration of Independence begins with justification for Revolution: Sometimes it becomes necessary to break with a nation with whom there is a political connection. They explain that humanity has certain inalienable rights (that should not be taken away) and governments were formed to protect these rights. (Remember chapter 1 and the cave men?) However, sometimes governments go bad and begin to take those rights away and because the people formed governments in the first place, they have the right to do away with a government that has gone bad and replace it with another government. (Pretty revolutionary stuff for sure.) It is made very clear in this document that a government should not be done away with for any old reason, only if it has been bad for some time. They realized the danger in the removal of a government and they make it clear that it is sometimes better to endure the mild injustices of a not-so-good situation. If you must do away with a government, a warning is given to make darn sure that you replace it with something that will endure. To justify the colonists' endeavor to replace the British government's control over them, they listed many actions on the part of the British government that showed that England fell into the category of a very bad government. The largest part of this document is taken up showing those wrongdoings. The document ends with a showing of good faith - that is to say, if England stopped doing those unjust things to the colonies, the colonists would once again be law abiding, king loving, loyal subjects. If the injustices persist, then the colonists would fight for their independence and in so doing they would pledge their lives, their fortunes and their sacred honor. The Declaration of Independence should be read at this time so that the beauty of the entire document could be impressed upon the reader once again.

Thus with this declaratory document justifying the reasons for our taking up of arms against the British, the American colonies marched further into war. The colonists were split about three ways so far as the their allegiances were concerned. There were the "Patriots," those who fought for independence - they comprised about one third of the population; there were those who endorsed or fought on the side of the British, referred to as the "Loyalists or Tories," that made up about one third of the colonial population and finally there were those who really didn't care one way or the other, or who would readily swing to the winning side, that figured in the final one third of the population of the colonies.

CHAPTER 3 WE GET ON OUR OWN

We had fought the strongest nation in the world and we won the war. England never brought its full power against us. We became an irritant to them and the idea that Englishmen were killing "Englishmen" did not make for a popular war back in Merry Old England. We had English advocates that spoke on our behalf in England. France helped us in this conflict not so much for the love of the Americans as it was for her dislike for the British. France had been pushed out of North America and it would make her heart glad to see the same happen to Great Britain. Finally, when George Washington whipped General Cornwallis at Yorktown, Virginia on October 17, 1781, the British called it quits.

We never brought Great Britain to her knees but because of the victories we did achieve, we made the British come to realize the futility of continuing the war. It seemed that an attitude of "good bye and good riddance" prevailed among some British hierarchy toward their North American possessions.

The colonies were likened to the dog that chases the automobile wheel: What is he going to do with it if he catches it? Here were the English colonies, very snug and secure under the protective blanket of one of the best and strongest governments in the world at that time. Now they must suffer the hard cold reality of independence. Once they got that autonomy, what were they going to do with it?

It must be noted that our push for independence caused Winston Churchill, the Prime Minister of Great Britain during World War II, to write that the first shot fired at Lexington - the shot that precipitated the American Revolution - was the "shot that was heard around the world." This phrase, taken from a song that was sung at the dedication of a battle monument at Concord on July 4, 1837, implied that we were the first to fight to win our independence when the world was completely dominated by mother countries possessing colonies around the world. Imperialism, the act of forming colonies, was the order of that day and we started something that would prevail throughout the 19th and 20th centuries. Today there are only a few colonies left in the world.

What was the reality of the newly acquired independence? The ex colonies were formed into a composite of thirteen individual, loosely knit states that had really never gotten along with one another except during the war itself. The states were jealous and suspicious of one another, they quarreled over possessions of Western lands and the smaller, weaker states feared the more powerful ones. As was mentioned, they did cooperate reasonably well during the British threat and the Continental Congress - as the central government was then called - had enough prestige to halfway get the job done. While the war was going on, a government was formed under a set of laws known as the Articles of Confederation. These articles set up a government based solely upon cooperation between the states. The states had complete sovereignty but cooperated with the other States to get a very important job done - that was to win the war.

THE ARTICLES OF CONFEDERATION

This document laid the foundation for the first Central Government under which the Americans lived upon winning their independence from the British. It was a loosely knit confederation of sovereign states that were controlled by their own state constitutions. Most all had governors to act as executives and had legislative bodies of one sort or another. Actually, the states were little countries unto themselves in all intent and purpose. They perceived the war they had just fought, not as an achievement of a central government but as a joint venture of individual states. They looked upon victory as each state winning all the freedoms, powers, privileges or "marbles." They had fought a long and bloody war to get rid of a strong central government and a king and they would not give up this newly won autonomy. They realized that they needed some kind of unity vested in a central government but they absolutely refused to give up their powers. What they got, as a result of this refusal, was a weak central government that was incapable of getting much done.

Suppose a person had the technology to build a Frankenstein monster. What kind of a monster would he build if he was aware of the outcome of the Frankenstein story - the monster ending up killing his creator? If he built a big, strong monster he could envision all the protection the monster could give him. He wouldn't have to lock his doors at night, or he could walk down the worse of the New York streets. This would be the epitome of protection, a "do it yourself" Incredible Hulk. Everything would be great except for that nagging feeling that someday this creature might turn against him.

The creator's other alternative is to build a monster only one foot high so that if it did turn against him, he could easily crush it. The trouble with this is, so could everyone else. Consequently, the one foot monster could not afford the man any protection whatsoever. This example brings into focus the difficulties of deciding what type of government one should build.

Before I attack the Articles of Confederation by mentioning all its weaknesses, I would like to mention a few positive things about the government which operated under it. It did carry us through the war. It borrowed and begged for money and it did keep the states in some type of order during these stressful times. After the war it did work on a peace treaty with Great Britain, it got the states to give up their rights to possessions of lands in the Northwest and it set up laws to govern those lands.

ONE GETS WHAT ONE PAYS FOR

Let us go through some of the provisions of the Articles of Confederation to get an understanding as to the reasons why they were weak. First of all, this document sets up a loose alliance among thirteen states. It possibly could have worked if the states had been able to get along better than they did. Congress could pass a law by an approval of nine of the thirteen states. Congress could not regulate trade between states and foreign nations. Congress had to beg money from the states and they could not tax to obtain money. There was no one to carry out the laws that were passed - no executive officer. Instead there was a committee that tried to run the business of government when Congress was not in session. I am reminded at this point of a camel. A camel is a horse that was put together by a committee. I never did check out the validity of that statement. (Some say that this committee type executive formed the basis of our cabinet system later.) The reason for this lack of an executive was the sour taste that remained of old King George III. The states weren't about to replace him with another. The new nation was reluctant to invest too much power into a federal government - the less power the better. That is exactly what they created; a "power-less" government.

It was down hill from then on. Several states claimed the territory of Vermont, a couple of states were about to go to war with one another over a dispute as to who owned the Potomac River. Money was printed with reckless abandon. The continental money was so worthless that a figure of speech was coined, "not worth a continental." - a description given to anything that was absolutely worthless. The states printed their own currency which caused a lot of confusion when they indulged in interstate commerce. The states set their own standard for weights and measurements which caused further confusion. Many states set up tariffs that had to be paid on goods coming across their borders. Debts could not be paid which in turn hurt our credit in domestic and foreign trade. Massachusetts was in rebellion, led by Daniel Shays, as a reaction to the courts taking away farms from those who could not meet their financial obligations. A few Americans longed for the "good old days" under British rule? Many were seriously contemplating asking England to take over again. Washington, long before, while the war was still in progress, was asked by his officers to take control of the country by force and to set himself up as a monarch. He reprimanded them royally for even thinking of such an idea.

When Great Britain and the victorious colonies sat down to write up a treaty, (Treaty of Paris) one provision on the part of the British was to remove their troops from the Great Lakes region. In another provision, the United States agreed to compensate for the loss of lands suffered by the Tories or Loyalists. John Adams, while in Great Britain as U.S. Diplomatic Envoy, asked a British official to remove the long overdue British troops from that area and to open certain ports that were agreed upon in the treaty, but were still not opened to U.S. shipping. Adams accused the British of not living up to the Treaty of Paris. The Britain reacted by accusing the United States Government of not living up to its commitments in the treaty by still not compensating the Tories for the loss of their lands. Adams tried to reassure his British counterpart that the United States government was doing everything that it could to see that the states obeyed this treaty. The British official, in a show of irritation and frustration, told Adams that the British government found it impossible to deal with an animal that had thirteen fists and no head. I think this says it all.

A government such as this would be considered a little odd in our day and time, but imagine how other countries looked upon this fledgling nation back in the eighteenth century. Almost every country in the world back then had some sort of king. It was accepted and very likely deemed necessary. Here were these weak, not wholly together, little pretentious group of states trying to exist without a king. "Why everybody has to have a king!" "Look around you!" "We all have kings!" said the world. Many countries were making book on the fact that these upstart united states would probably have a king before long.

THE CONSTITUTIONAL CONVENTION

In the mist of all this chaos a group of men from various states felt that the only salvation for this foundering nation was to form a wholly different government - one that would have the proper power to get things done. These people were labeled Federalists because of their desire to bring about a stronger federal government. They had to approach the American people cautiously because of the general fear among the populace of a strong central government.

The opportunity arose when a meeting was called at Washington's house to try to solve a problem between Virginia and Maryland over the use of the Potomac River. At this meeting another meeting was called for the following year at Annapolis, Maryland. At the meeting in Annapolis, it was decided to meet again the following year at Philadelphia, Pennsylvania for the purpose of strengthening the Articles of Confederation. Most everyone agreed that the federal government needed some readjustment in order for the country to survive. The Federalists pushed for this meeting under the pretext of "putting more teeth" into the Articles of Confederation. If they had said anything at that time about the idea of replacing the document completely, many would not have shown up for that next meeting. The delegates met in Philadelphia for the purpose of revising the Articles and when they arrived there they were hit right between the eyes with a new idea: Let's get rid of the Articles of Confederation and begin a new document entirely.

This meeting was called during the summer months of 1787. In order to create a situation whereby the delegates could speak openly, without the fear of public ridicule and pressure, it was decided to hold the proceedings in private. In so doing the windows and the doors were closed to the public. It was the practice of the day, before radio or television, for people who were interested, to stand outside of buildings where meetings were held, listening through the open windows. One can imagine the discomfort felt by the delegates sitting in this sweltering Philadelphia summer heat without electric fans or airconditioning, with clothing not made as comfortably as today.

One of the youngest men there was tagged with the title "The Father of the American Constitution." James Madison, would later become a President of the United States. He was responsible for letting the world know exactly what took place at this convention by writing a journal of the proceedings. (Remember it was a secret meeting.) Madison described how he positioned himself in such an area so that he could hear the delegates from the rear of the room as well as from the front. He gained this title of "Father" many years after when he became older.

It would be fair to say that there was heat present at this convention in greater quantity than what the hot summer months could produce. This heat became evident as the delegates quarreled through many meetings. There were so many different people from so many different states with so many different opinions, all of which were more than one could imagine. They brought to this gathering the fears, jealousies, and mistrust of one state for another; the fears of small states toward big states and the apprehension toward the common people. Concerns over large government and state economies prevailed in their arguments and discussions. There were the ever-present strong government advocates opposed to the states righters and the question of slavery reared its ugly head many times.

One big disagreement that deadlocked the convention was the problem of representation. In this controversy the big states and the little states (population wise) came into direct opposition to one another. The small states, fearing that they would become victim to the desires of the larger states, were emphatic in their demands that each state have an equal vote in deciding laws, as was the case under the Articles of Confederation. The larger states felt this to be unfair because of their larger populations. These larger states argued that the people in the smaller states would have an unfair advantage because fewer people would have the luxury of a representative, whereas in the larger states, a representative would have to share his time and talents among many, many more constituents. It seemed that the convention could not get over this hump. The delegates were hopelessly deadlocked and were about to head back to their homes. A solution did come about and with hindsight, it seems a very simple solution - however, someone had to came up with it first. With this dead-lock broken it was possible for the convention to get on with other business. When Article One is reviewed in a later chapter, that very simple solution will be brought to light.

Another big disagreement that ran rampant at that convention was over how big a part were the common people to play. You must consider the cautious approach to common people against the backdrop of the 18th century. "Common people" of today have the advantage of education whereas two hundred years ago the common people were not educated and acted in that manner. A popular belief of the middle ages, that was lodged in the minds of many more fortunate individuals of the upper classes, was the idea that common people were thus because they did not possess in their character the attributes necessary to lift them from their "commonness." A residue of this medieval approach to common man still was with many of the delegates. They mistrusted common people and believed that they should have as little to do with government as possible. An example of how they believed can be seen in this modern day statement. "You wouldn't allow your six year old nephew to take your new Cadillac out for a spin would you?" The desire to deprive the common people the privileges under a new government was not the question. Every one should benefit, however not everyone should participate. This concept seems incompatible with our ideas of democracy, but many of the "middle class" Americans, at that time, participated in government, with a feeling of the old European concept of "Noblesse Oblige." (A feeling of obligation on the part of the nobility to work for and to take care of his government, which in turn would benefit the common man.) One "pro common man" delegate included in his argument that, "The pyramid of our government should be built so high that it would need a very broad base upon which to be founded." (This meant that the common people should be included.) Immediately, an "anti-common man" advocate, stood up and shouted, "No, No, the people should have as little to do with this government as possible, they lack for information and are easily misled." One can see evidence in this delegate of a fear of demagoguery, that is to say a possibility that someday a fast talking, flashy type person, using the ignorance of the populace could gain control of the country. This has happened more than once in the history of our planet. The word "Democracy" was not too popular a term among the middle class at that time. It was too much associated with radical concepts and was sometimes feared. The word "republic" was much more in keeping with the views of the times. The use of the word "democracy" will become popular later in our history and would be used profusely.

Thomas Jefferson believed in the potential of the common man. He felt that common man had the ability to participate in government and hold office but education was foremost a requirement. Jefferson advocated public education very enthusiastically. It should be noted that Jefferson played no direct part in this Constitutional Convention since he was in France as an official of the U.S. Government. Had he been here he would not have been too much in favor of a strong federal government because he feared it, as did Patrick Henry and many others at that time. It will not be revealed in this chapter the outcome of this "common man" controversy. All this disagreement over common people and the amount of participation allowed them will come to light when Article I of the Constitution is reviewed in another chapter .

The question of slavery needed also to be resolved. This was a hot potato and as little that was said or done about it the better. A hot potato was handed me as a teacher every time one of my Black students would question the validity of the Declaration of Independence as the statement, "All men are created equal, etc." was read and the Constitution and Bill of Rights was studied. The only answer I could give them was that they had to look upon these documents in the setting of the 18th century and the fact that many delegates owned slaves at the time that they upheld that "all men were created equal." I had to be honest with them. The Black man was not even considered in the spectrum of "men" as the framers considered men's equality. The good news for the Black man came later as a direct force of that Constitution as it employed its capability of interpretation and change through the years. It took the death of many in a Civil War and the sacrifice of many people, Black and White to bring about these changes. It was the potential of the Constitution that made it possible for this change and because of interpretation and amendments, this document now includes them as well. I tried to explain to them that man, not the document, was at fault for the inequities of the past. At times it seemed that this answer did not do the trick, but it was the best that I had to offer and I gave it my best shot. One does see a compromise over the question of slavery in Article One, enough to satisfy the delegates in 1787 but not the Black student of today. This solution will also be brought to light when Article One is studied.

Other differences had to be resolved. The delegates had to work on problems concerning sectionalism, economics and many other things. When the various articles and clauses are discussed, I will refer to certain situations, problems and compromises that brought those articles and clauses into existence in the Constitution. One thing that impresses me about this document is that it came into existence in spite of all the differences that were obviously present.

CHAPTER 4 THE CONSTITUTION

THE STRUCTURE

Structurally speaking, the Constitution is divided into three basic parts: 1. The Preamble which states the purpose for the existence of the Constitution. 2. The main body that is made up of seven articles which in turn are broken down into sections and clauses. These articles and sections are numbered so that they can readily be found or identified. 3. The amendments which were added to the Constitution after it was put into effect. They are called Articles but may be called Amendments. The amendments are identified by the number. After the first ten, our Bill of Rights, the number indicates the sequence in which the amendment was incorporated into the document. The amendments are also broken down into sections and clauses.

A CONSTITUTION DEFINED

A Constitution can be defined as a blueprint for setting up a government. It can be considered a contract between the people and the government that it creates. It can be a set of rules under which a people operate, or a set of rules that determine the type of laws that can or cannot be made. It can determine the behavior and the limitations under which the people or the officials can operate within the system. It can become a symbol of unity for a nation, especially during war or troubled times. The expression used in oaths such as "to defend the Constitution" becomes synonymous with defending the country itself. Our Constitution can become a cloak or shield, especially the Bill of Rights, in protecting an individual against the awesome power of government, if that government should ever turn against that individual.

THE PREAMBLE

The direct translation for the word preamble is "to walk before." The Preamble simply comes before the Constitution and explains the purpose of the Constitution. (A copy of the Constitution can be found almost anywhere. The Preamble should be read at this time so that a feeling for the mood of the delegates, two hundred years past, can be made manifest.)

In effect the Preamble is saying: We Americans are creating this Constitution in order to have a better government than what we had under the Articles of Confederation. We are creating a better government for the purpose of: establishing justice; making sure that we have peace within our land; defending ourselves from all enemies; providing for the needs of the people and making sure that freedom continues for ourselves and for those who come after us (this means the people of today as well as one hundred years from now).

THE MAIN BODY

The main body has seven Articles. The first three Articles deal with the creation of the actual government itself. The government had to be brought into existence before anything else within the Constitution could be put into effect.

ARTICLE I THE LEGISLATIVE BRANCH

Section 1 Sets up a two House legislative (law making) system called Congress. It is composed of the House of Representatives and the Senate.

Section 2 Established the House of Representatives.

Section 3 Established the Senate.

(Sections 2 and 3 elaborate upon the uniqueness of each House so far as qualifications and certain duties that each has that the other does not have. For the remainder of Article I, all the sections are involved with the duties and responsibilities of both Houses acting together as the Congress of the United States. It should also be noted that this Article is the longest in the Constitution.)

Sections 4 to 10 explain the powers and duties of the Congress of the United States. It also states the powers that are prohibited by the Congress.

ARTICLE II THE EXECUTIVE BRANCH

Section 1 The President of the United States stands at the head of this branch. This section sets forth the qualifications for a person who aspires to become a president, how he is to be elected, the oath of office that he takes, and the president's salary.

Section 2 Lists the powers of the President.

Section 3 Lists the duties that he must undertake.

Section 4 States the procedure for the removal of a president and other high officials.

ARTICLE III THE JUDICIAL BRANCH

Section 1 sets up the Supreme Court as head of the Judicial Branch. It will be the top federal court in the land and it states that the lesser federal courts shall be established by the Congress of the United States.

Section 2 Deals with the Jurisdiction of Federal Courts.

Section 3 Defines treason. This label cannot be arbitrarily used against a citizen.

ARTICLE 4 THE RELATIONSHIPS

This article establishes a relationship between the states, as well as a relationship between the states and the federal government.

Section 1 Tells how official records will be regarded.

Section 2 Lists certain privileges of citizens.

Section 3 Opens the door to new states and territories.

Section 4 Lists some guarantees that the states have.

ARTICLE 5 AMENDING THE CONSTITUTION

Article 5 determines the method by which the Constitution can be altered or changed. It is no easy task to bring about a Constitutional change.

ARTICLE 6 CATCH ALL PROVISIONS

It seemed that all the things they had laying around and did not know what to do with they put into this Article.

Section 1 Promises that all prior debts will be paid.

Section 2 Ascertains that this document is the supreme law of the land.

Section 3 Necessitates oaths of office.

ARTICLE 7 RATIFICATION

This article accomplished one task and one task alone and that was to set up the means for ratification. Once accomplished, it just sits there not doing anything.

THE AMENDMENTS

AMENDMENTS 1 THROUGH 10 (THE BILL OF RIGHTS)

Amendment 1 Freedom of Religion, Speech, Assembly and Petition. (This amendment is the biggie!)

Amendment 2 The right to bear arms. This one is the National Riflemen's Association's pride and joy.

Amendment 3 Quartering of soldiers. This one doesn't stir up much excitement.

Amendment 4 Search and Seizure. "We have here a warrant for your arrest." say the T.V. detective stories.

Amendment 5 Rights of those accused of a crime. Some of my students really knew this one. As soon as the cuffs go "click," you begin to relate to the fifth amendment.

Amendment 6 Rights in a jury trial. You can check out all the TV shows about court room trials. There will be many of them.

Amendment 7 Civil cases. There are many cases involving suits between various parties. Our courts are loaded with these.

Amendment 8 No excessive bail nor cruel and unusual punishment. Does the death penalty of the several states contradict this amendment?

Amendment 9 Powers kept by the people. There exists more rights that the people have that are not mentioned in the Constitution.

Amendment 10 Powers reserved by the states. All powers that the Federal Government possess were once given to it by the states. However, the states did keep some of these powers for themselves.

AMENDMENTS 11 - 26 Brought into the Constitution as a need for them arose in American history. The study of these articles is in actuality a study of American History itself.

Amendment 11 The manner by which citizens and foreigners will sue the state governments and the U.S. Government.

Amendment 12 Elections of presidents and vice presidents. Political parties and common people have played a much greater role than anticipated.

The 13th, 14th, and 15th amendments are referred to as the Post Civil War Amendments. These amendments address themselves to Blacks and guided the United States to a greater role in democracy.

Amendment 13 The abolition of slavery. No more involuntary servitude in the United States, except as punishment for a crime.

Amendment 14 Rights of citizens. A lengthy amendment and like Article VI, is a catch-all for several unrelated clauses.

Amendment 15 Former slaves now have the right to vote. One of the most abused amendments. For many years this amendment was violated.

Amendment 16 The Citizens get the privilege to pay income tax.

Amendment 17 Senators are now elected by the people. At the beginning the people only voted for their representatives.

Amendment 18 The prohibition amendment. No more alcoholic beverages in the United States. A noble experiment. This also will be abused.

Amendment 19 Women's right to vote. Many women in the United States fought long and hard for this privilege. The fight still goes on for other denied rights of women.

Amendment 20 A change in the date for federal elections. The Lame Duck Amendment. Modern communication and transportation mandated a change - thus this amendment.

Amendment 21 Alcohol became legal again. The noble experiment failed. People would not stop drinking. We learned the lesson that laws cannot be passed to regulate morality.

Amendment 22 A time limit is placed on how long a president was to stay in office. This was a reaction to Roosevelt's four terms.

Amendment 23 People in Washington D.C. can now vote in presidential elections.

Amendment 24 No more poll tax. This was a convenient method of abusing Amendment 15. It kept people from voting.

Amendment 25 The procedure used by which a vice president can take over in a situation other than the death of a president.

Amendment 26 Lowering of the voting age from 21 to 18. The logic being, if you are old enough to go to war at 18 you are certainly old enough to vote.

In later chapters we will take each of these amendments and find out the reasons for their existence and the results of their presence within the Constitution of the United States.

CHAPTER 5 THE LEGISLATIVE BRANCH

ARTICLE I THE CONGRESS OF THE UNITED STATES

(The longest article in the Constitution.)
Sections 1, 2 and 3

In chapter three it was mentioned how the big disagreement over representation put the convention in a hopeless deadlock. The small states wanted equal representation and the large states wanted representation to be based upon the amount of people within the state. A very simple solution was brought forth which broke the deadlock and allowed the delegates to go on to other things. The solution was to give both the large and small states what they wanted. This is known in constitutional history as the "Great Compromise." A "compromise" is a method by which an agreement is reached by both sides giving up a little. The compromise was to create a bicameral (two House) legislature. The Senate would have equal representation - this gave the small states what they wanted. The membership of the House of Representatives would be based upon the amount of people living within a state - this of course would satisfy the large states. This arrangement would be satisfactory to both sides, because any bill under consideration would have to be passed by both of these Houses. It is highly suggested that Article I be looked over at this time to get a better "feeling" for this document.

Section 1 CONGRESS

Section 1 sets up two law making bodies. It states that all the power to make laws shall be vested in a body called Congress which will be composed of a Senate and a House of Representatives.

The duties of both the Senate and House of Representatives are basically the same, however the few differences that each have will be mentioned in Section 2, concerning the House of Representatives and Section 3 which concerns the Senate.

Section 2 THE HOUSE OF REPRESENTATIVES

Section 2 deals with the House of Representatives. In referring back to chapter three, mention was made of the lack of faith that many of the middle and upper class had toward the people of the lower class. It must be stressed at this point that the House of Representative was the only organ that had direct responsibility to the people. The people of each state could vote for a representative and that official represented and answered directly to the people. These representatives received the title "Congressmen." Electing members of the House of Representatives was the extent of the voting privileges of the people, so far as the federal government was concerned at that time in history. It will be noted as we go through Article I, that ordinary people did not vote for senators nor presidents. The qualifications for voting, as determined by the states, were that you were adult, white, male and owned property - this excluded many people. It was felt that a person who did not own property would not have enough at stake to vote responsibly. As more people moved to the cities and lived in apartments the property ownership prerequisite became less important. The qualification for voting was left to the states to determine. The United States Constitution made sure that the same qualifications that the states had for elections within the state governments be also applied in federal elections.

A person must be aware that democracy, as we know it today, was not automatically materialized at the strokes of the delegates pens on the final days of the convention. Democracy, as we know it, was a growing thing that developed through the good and bad times of our existence. Democracy as we know it, did not come cheaply. It was paid for, and is still being paid for by the blood, sweat, tears and hard work of many Americans. Our Democracy is a growing thing that will continue to grow as our country grows. If it stopped growing we would surely die as a democratic nation.

Members of the House of Representatives will be elected in a staggered manner so that half of the members from any state will not be up for election in the same year. There will always be a minimum of one year experience within the membership of a state.

A term of office for a representative is two years. The delegates felt that in order for the people to control a representative he must have the specter of re-election staring him in the face constantly. In modern times some feel that the length of the term of office should be increased because of the large expense of campaigning. A congressmen no sooner gets elected when he is faced with the burden of campaigning again.

In order to qualify as a candidate for the House of Representatives, a person must be at least twenty five years of age and a citizen of the United States for the last seven years and must be a resident of the state that he wishes to represent. The constitutional qualifications for office are few, however the American voters demand that men and women running for office have a lot more going for them than what are listed as qualifications within the Constitution. Great expense is utilized in shaping the candidate's image to meet the standards of the American voters for a certain election year. Media campaigns are placed into the hands of men who have advertising experience and candidates are displayed to the public with the same expertise as selling canned goods and soap.

As already stated, the number of representatives that a state will have depends upon the amount of people living within a state. Thus the expression: "representation will be based upon population." The idea as originally put forward was to add representatives as the population of the state increased. After accumulating 435 House members it was decided that the chamber was getting a little overcrowded so now the membership remains at 435. As states gain or lose people, representatives are taken from those states losing and given to those states gaining population.

A counting of heads - a census - is taken every ten years to determine the amount of people in a state so that the states would receive their share of representatives. Although the head count of people in the United States is used to determine many things in our government, the constitutional justification for the census is for determining representation.

It must be further noted that many clauses within the Constitution are no longer in effect because of amendments being added through the years. There are a few in Section 2.

In chapter 3, reference was made of the little done about slavery during the time of the Convention. Several clauses did refer to slavery, but being the hot potato that it was, as little was said as possible to please as many delegates as possible. The South which had most of the slave population wanted the best of two worlds. When it came to determining how much tax a state should pay, the Southern States did not want to count their slaves because the amount of taxes that a state paid was determined by the population of the states. However, when it came to determining how many representatives a state should have, the Southern States wanted to include their slaves in the count. The North, having fewer slaves, felt this to be unfair. The convention went round and round on this point until another compromise was reached. It was called the "Three-fifths Compromise" which allowed the Southern States to count three- fifths of their slaves in determining the population count for both taxation and representation. This compromise no longer applies as a result of the 13th Amendment.

The Constitution actually tells how many representatives a state should have based on a figure of 30,000 people per member and lists each state and their total representatives. This is no longer in effect as population constantly grew to render the listing as obsolete.

Several more things should be brought to light about Section 2 before we leave it. In case a congressman dies the governor of that state will choose a replacement until such time as an election can be held.

The House of Representatives will elect a Speaker of the House and other officers. In case a president and a vice president die in the same term, it is the Speaker of the House who will become the President. (This is not covered in the Constitution but by act of Congress.) This House also has the power to run its own meeting and set its own rules. It also has the sole power of impeachment - that is, to bring charges against any high official for wrongdoing. Impeachment will be discussed in Section 3.

Tax bills can originate only in the House of Representatives. More detail about taxation will be elaborated upon in Section 7 of this article.

SECTION 3 THE SENATE

Section 3 The Senate was an organ whose members originally represented and were elected by the state governments. As years passed the Senate slowly assumed the responsibility of representing the people of the state along with the state governments. It would not be until the present century that an amendment would be passed to allow the people to directly vote for their Senators.

There are two Senators from each state, each having one vote and a term of six years. Every three years an election will be held in a state for the office of Senator so that a situation will not exist whereby two senators will be running for office from the same state at the same time. This is designed so that one Senator from a state will have at least a total of three years experience, and one Senator can mind the store while the other campaigns.

The qualifications for a Senator is that he has reached the age of thirty years, that he has been a citizen of the United States for a total of nine years prior to running for Senator and that he is a resident of the state that he wishes to represent.

The Vice President of the United States presides over the Senate, because he is the President of the Senate. He can vote only to break a tie and when he is not present he is replaced by a President Pro Tempore (Pro Tem) - a temporary president. The Senate is responsible for electing all the other officers of that chamber.

Impeachment trials are held in the Senate. Remember, impeachment charges are brought forth by the House of Representatives and the Senate is responsible for trying these wrong-doing high officials. In case of an impeachment trial involving the President, the Supreme Court Chief Justice will preside over the trial, instead of the Vice President. It seem that the outcome of an impeachment trial involving the President would effect the career of the Vice President too greatly - he obviously could not be too objective in his duties as the presiding officer no matter how hard he tried. The only outcome of an impeachment conviction is removal from office. An impeached official could then be tried in a criminal court and be punished upon being found guilty, if the situation was deemed warranted. Errant Senators and Representatives are not impeached. Instead they are removed from their seats in Congress by the powers of removal within their respective Houses.

The Senate, in a sense, seems to be more prestigious than the House of Representatives. The qualifications are slightly higher and in the beginning, Senators represented their state governments. The very fact that there are 100 Senators as opposed to 435 House members makes for a feeling of more prestige so far as Senators are concerned. As individuals advance in government, it is the movement from the House of Representatives to the Senate and usually not the other way around. For presidential hopefuls out there, a good road to that office is from the House to the Senate to the Oval Office.

The remainder of the sections in Article I will refer to the Congress of the United States which will include both the Senate and the House of Representatives.

CHAPTER 6

THE CONGRESS OF THE UNITED STATES

Sections 4 to 10 deal with Congress as it applies to both Houses. There are a few differences between the Houses and they were dealt with specifically in Sections 2 and 3. For the remainder of Article I both Houses will be dealt with as the unit known as the Congress of the United States.

SECTION 4 ELECTIONS AND MEETINGS

The time, place and manner of electing members of the U.S. Congress is determined by the state legislature of each specific state. However, Congress can change all except the locations of the voting areas by law. One interpretation for disallowing Congress to change the location of voting areas within a state is to insure that the states can conveniently place voting booths so that their people can vote in national elections. It would keep a wayward Congress from passing a law to place voting booths at such an inconvenience that people would be kept from voting their "uncooperative" Congressmen out of office.

One thing you will notice about our Constitution, there was in the back of the minds of a lot of delegate, the fear that a government could go bad at anytime and they placed as many safeguards as they could think of in this document. I will give many examples of the checks and balances in our system from time to time.

Congress must meet at least once a year. During the pre revolutionary period the British Parliament closed down the legislative body of, to name just one, Massachusetts - if you remember your history, this body, as a result of this shutdown, met in the local tap room to conduct its business. The little clause ordering Congress to meet once a year, gives our Legislature the Constitutional right to assemble. If ever the country got into a situation whereby pressure was put upon the Congress in such a way that they could not assemble to carry out their duties for the benefit of the American people, the second clause in Section 4, Article I would give the Congress the Constitutional authority to override such a mandate. Once assembled they could set up their own rules to meet regularly.

SECTION 5 RULES FOR CONDUCTING BUSINESS

Each House will judge their election returns and qualifications for its members. A majority will constitute a quorum (the amount of members necessary to conduct business) and members may be forced to attend a meeting to establish a quorum.

Each House may determine its own rules, punish its members and with a two-third vote, expel a member. Legislators are not impeached, rather a wrong doing member of the House or Senate can be expelled by their respective House.

Each House will keep a journal of its proceedings which will be published from time to time, except those things requiring secrecy. Congressional records are also published of everyday business of both Houses and are easily accessible through libraries and other sources. Everything is placed within this record. If a member gives a speech, recites a poem, or reads a passage from a book, etc cetera - all that will be placed within the record. Most of the time it makes for boring reading and takes a very dedicated soul to read it. However at times, especially when something great is going down, these Congressional Records can become very interesting. If one-fifth of the members present approve, the "yeas" or "nays" of the members on a certain issue can be recorded for everyone to see.

Neither House during a session can adjourn for more then three days or move to another location without the other House approving. (This is another safeguard)

SECTION 6 PRIVILEGES RESTRICTIONS

Congress can determine by law what their own salaries are. This could be a very convenient situation for our lawmakers. Fortunately for the taxpayer, the Congressmen are held in check by fear of repercussion from their constituents and from the public in general. Every time they try to legislate a large pay raise the country seems to go wild in protest. When there is legislation to increase the salaries of other office holders, it seems that the reaction isn't as great. It must be the fact that they are capable of legislating a raise for themselves that makes the difference. In the Primary Florida gubernatorial race of 1990 there was a campaign going on between two U.S. Senators for the office of governor. Part of the strategy of one candidate was his accusation that his opponent voted in favor of a pay hike for legislators, and of course, he in turn voted against it. I used this example to prove the point that should Senators or House members vote for a pay raise, it could come back to haunt them. Congress will be paid from the Treasury of the United States.

Except in cases of treason, felony or breach of peace, legislators cannot be arrested during a session, nor going to and from a session. You could imagine a situation where other government officials could try to stop certain members of Congress from influencing Congress against passing "unfavorable" laws by throwing those "uncooperative" members in jail. Another guarantee in this clause is the declaration that what is said in Congress can be said freely and without fear of retribution. A member of either House can not hold any other government job while he is serving his term. When he is no longer a member of Congress, he shall not be allowed to hold any government job that was created, or an increase of salary voted upon, when he was a member of Congress. This is to keep a Congressmen or Senator from helping to create a lucrative job and then taking advantage of that job when he is no longer in Congress.

SECTION 7 HOW LAWS ARE PASSED

All tax bills shall originate in the House of Representatives, but the Senate must concur and offer amendments to the bill as they can do on other bills. This is an interesting clause with a lot of historical significance. I hope that it has not been so long a time since the reader studied American History or seen stories about this situation on film, that he cannot remember one of the mottos of the pre Revolutionary War era: "No taxation without representation!" Taxation itself wasn't the entire issue at that time. The colonist did not entirely resent paying taxes. I imagine they grumbled as we do today, but they realized the necessity of being taxed. The tea tax that they so violently protested was imposed on them by a "fair minded" British Parliament who felt that the colonists surely would not resent a tax on an article that was actually cheaper to buy in the colonies than it was in England. The actual protestation against taxation was that these tax laws were legislated, in a far removed Parliament, some 3000 miles away - away from any form of representation. Our founding fathers still had a bad taste in their mouths over this taxation situation when they were forming the Constitution. They made sure that only our Representatives could initiate any bill that would hit Americans squarely in the pocket book.

It would be too lengthy a process to describe in all its detail how a bill becomes a law. This could be a volume in itself. There are a few things to note, however, as the Constitution spells them out, and a few things that are not spelled out in this document. One fact worth mentioning, that is not specifically stated, is that only Congressmen can introduce a bill (a proposed law) into the House and only a Senator can introduce a bill in the Senate. Even the president does not have that privilege. A president usually courts certain legislators and will influence them to submit bills on his behalf. The people working through various associations and pressure groups will have members of either House submit bills for them. We have the time honored "Lobbyists" who will constantly try to exert pressure on legislators to have bills introduced to benefit the companies and associations that the Lobbyists represent. They are called by this name because they are not allowed in the Chambers - the Lobby is as "fur as they kin git."

A bill is passed by both Houses with a majority vote. If both Houses approve, it must then go to the president for his approval. If the president approves it, it becomes a law when he signs it. If he vetoes (Latin: I forbid) the bill, it does not become a law unless it can be passed by two--thirds of both Houses. The bill will then become a law over the president's veto. Historically, only a small percentage of bills have been passed into law over a presidential veto because a two-thirds vote is hard to come by in Congress. If a president does not sign or veto the bill, it will become a law within 10 working days of Congress. President Andy Jackson used this method called the "pocket veto" extensively. It seems that traditionally, Congress uses up most of its time getting all the little piddling, insignificant bills out of the way and the "biggies" are saved until last. (This is the time that the Congressional Records become more interesting to read.) When these few very important bills are placed on the president's desk there usually are not ten working days left in the session of Congress. By not taking this action, the president can stop some of the bills that he deems to be unfavorable.

SECTION 8 THE POWERS THAT CONGRESS HAS

This section sets forth the powers of the Congress of the United States. The powers of Congress are those powers that the states gave to the Federal Government.

Congress has the power to tax and collect taxes, pay debts and provide for the defense and general welfare. (Remember, only the House of Representatives can initiate a tax bill.) This clause also declares that all tax laws must be uniform in every state throughout the United States.

Congress can borrow money on credit from the United States. Congress can borrow money from other countries and from its own citizens. One interesting way of borrowing money from U.S. citizens is through the sale of bonds. (They have been called War Bonds, Defense Bonds, Victory Bonds, Saving Bonds, etc depending upon the era that the bonds were sold.) During times of crises, great appeals were made to the patriotism of a person to purchase these bonds. A bond was bought with the idea that after a period of time that bond would be redeemed for more money because of an accumulation of interest.

The clause that sets forth the idea that Congress has the power to regulate foreign and interstate commerce is one of the most important clauses in the entire Constitution so far as the accumulation of power by the Federal government is concerned. It deserves a lot of space for clarification. In essence, this clause says that because Congress can control anything that concerns the buying and selling and moving of goods and services from one state to another, it opens up the door to tremendous power. Just about any type of activity that takes place between one state and another usually involves commerce. When this document was written, most all the activity involving interstate commerce dealt with roads, wagons and sailing vessels. As our technology advanced, after the writing of the Constitution, trains, trucks, planes, telephones, radio and television came into existence. It was easy to interpret the interstate commerce clause to include these new advances because, in effect these technical advances were involved with interstate commerce. Let me state some examples: As the railroads grew and flourished the owners of these companies began to look and act like gods that issued forth their own commercial commandments. They took advantage of America and its people. It became time for the American people to say, "enough is enough" to the railroad magnates. The people looked toward the

Federal government to do something about the high cost of railroad use and misuse and railroad safety.

Congress took on the job of taking some of the wind out of the sails of the railroad magnates. Nowhere in the Constitution did it say that Congress could control railroads, but there it was - Article I, Section 8, Clause 3; "Congress has the power to regulate interstate commerce" and is not the railroad involved in interstate commerce? The same became true with the regulation of aircraft, telephones, radio and TV. All those mentioned are involved with interstate commerce. As aircraft became more plentiful, a danger became evident in the skies. It was congress that began to set up rules and regulations to restore order and safety in the skies by legislating government agencies into existence to handle these things. If the Star Trek method of transportation ever became a reality, presumably, the Congress of the United States would be able to control the amount of power that the transporters has, set the standards for the transporter rooms, license those doing the transporting and establish the "Molecular Disassembly/Assembly Transportation Commission."

It should be well noted that our Federal Government expanded, not through a process of blatant usurpation on the part of the Federal Government itself, but because of the insistence on the part of the American people for the federal government to take charge. The first line of defense, the state governments, where, traditionally the people would go to have a problem rectified, were reluctant or unable to satisfy many of the needs of their people.

Congress can make laws which would determine how non-citizens can become citizens of the United States. They can also set up standards for bankruptcy. Mention is made of the fact that these laws must be uniform throughout the United States.

Congress can coin (print) and regulate the value of domestic and foreign money. They determine our weights and measurements. They have the authority as to what a pound, ton, inch and foot are. Legislation was passed within the last generation to have the metric system side by side with our own method of weights and measurements. That is why some of our things are measured in liters and meters.

Laws would be passed to deal with the punishment of counterfeiters of securities and money. The Constitution mentions only three crimes specifically: counterfeiting, piracy and treason. Piracy will be dealt with in clause 10 of this section and treason will be discussed in Article III, The Judicial Branch.

Congress has the authority to set up post offices and post roads. The Massachusetts Colony established the first post office in 1639. Mother England ran the postal service in the American Colonies from 1707 until the War for Independence. During the war, our postal service was created with Benjamin Franklin as the first Post Master General. Upon the establishment of the postal service under this clause our nation had seventy-five local post offices. Adhesive stamps introduced in 1874 simplified the mailing of letters.

Changes took place in our country when the post office began to deliver mail to the farms in 1896. This was known as R.F.D. or rural free delivery. This new mail service brought forth another type of retail business. Great catalogue houses such as Montgomery Ward sprang up to supply a new convenient method of shopping through rural free delivery. The catalogue became second to the Bible to many farmers who used it to "shop at home" by mail and it also served a purpose in the outhouse.

Congress has the power to promote the progress of science and useful arts by giving the creators and their descendants the exclusive rights to their creations for a given time. This would aid in providing the creators of art and science a chance at recognition and financial gain, which in turn would increase the incentive for originating new things. Thus our patent and copyright laws.

As mandated in Article III, The Judicial Branch, Congress has the power to set up lessor (inferior) courts to the Supreme Courts. This they have done by creating appellate and federal district courts throughout the United States.

The definition and the punishment for piracy and felonies on the high seas would be determined by Congress. It seemed logical that the framers at the convention realized that crimes committed within the states were within the jurisdiction of the states and did not need to be covered in the Constitution. However, here was a situation whereby the state governments would have no jurisdiction. Laws, therefore, would have to be made to take care of these extra-state felonies.

Congress has the power to declare war. The last declared war that the United States fought was World War II. Korea, Vietnam, and a few of the skirmishes we have had along the way since World War II were brought about by a president using his powers as Commander-in-Chief of the Armed Forces. He has the power to meet emergencies by calling out troops. After two long wars fought through the use of presidential "police power," Congress has reacted by passing a law which limits a presidential police action to a specified number of days.

Congress has the power to grant *Letters of Marque*; a special commission for private ship captains to attack ships of a designated country. (Usually an enemy of the country issuing this commission.) This portion of "the right of Congress to declare war" clause is outdated, but at the time of the framing this "Letter" granting was an accepted activity among many other countries and paved the way for certain "privateers" of note in world history. There have been many films made about the adventures of pirates and privateer and buccaneers through the years and many are cluttering up the networks on TV. The names "pirates, privateers and buccaneers" seems to confuse many people and some think that they are the same. There is a difference however. The privateer has the *Letter of Marque* and attacks ships of a designated country. He has a home base in which to return, namely the country from which he was offered the *Letter of Marque*. The pirate attacks ships of all nations indiscriminately and has no home port in any country. A Buccaneer is almost the same as a pirate and is entirely too expensive for corn. (A little humor inserted here.)

Congress controls the money to maintain an army and a navy. Money can be appropriated for only two years at a time. When the Constitutional "checks and balance system" is discussed, I will use this control as one of its prime examples by stating that the President is Commander-in-Chief of the Armed Forces but he could not move those forces one mile without the money that he gets from Congress.

Congress can make up the rules for the government and regulations of the Army and Navy. Upon entering a branch of the military service, a person finds that he has signed a paper stating that he is now under the United States Code of Military Justice.

Congress provides for a militia and can call for them in time of emergencies. The idea of a militia goes back to the very beginning of the colonization of our land. If the settlers had bonafide professional soldiers to protect them, everything was fine. In most cases there were not enough of, or no military personnel around to protect the settlers in what were very dangerous times. Indians were the order of the day and usually, because of the misdeeds of the settlers themselves, these natives were unfriendly and sometimes downright hostile. The settlers had themselves, their families and their land to protect and the task of doing this fell entirely into their own hands. Some sort of a plan was mapped out in an area. Sometimes a fortification was erected and a signal was created as a warning of eminent danger. When a fort cannon was fired it could be a signal for all the outlying homesteads to heed. All the families and what they could carry in the time they had, rushed to the fort for safety. As the children and the women were put into a relatively safe place, the men formed into a fighting force. This was the reason for the beginning of the militia. As time went by, the militia became more sophisticated and actually were very efficient at times. These militiamen played an important role in the French and Indian war. Remember, George Washington was a colonel in the Virginia Militia. What can be said that hasn't been said about the part the militiamen played in the Revolutionary War? Many of the Northern Militia came South at the beginning of the Civil War, all enthusiastic and bedecked in their very colorful state militia uniforms, as though going to a parade, only to find that the war was not going to be a picnic.

The term "militia" died out and in its place we now have the National Guard and the Reserves. The idea behind the Reserves and National Guard is the realization that a large standing army in peace is not logical. The expense of having an army, large enough to meet any enemy, just waiting around in case a war breaks out, is very impractical. One reason for the outbreak of World War I was the fact that these principal nations had large standing armies. Countries as well as individuals do not start fights when they think that they are too weak to whip the other side. Sometimes, ideas tried and tested are the best, and our "militia system" has been around and working successfully for a long time.

We use the old ways that settlers protected themselves by having a number of citizens trained so that in time of war or emergencies these "citizen soldiers" or "weekend warriors" along with the professional army already in existence, can become the first line of defense until the government can mobilize a wartime army through the draft system. These National Guard units in each state are controlled by the executive officer (governor) of that state and can be called out to meet state emergencies. Congress supplies the money for these units as stated in the Constitution. In case of war or other emergencies, the national guard and reserve units are called up by the Congress of the United States and they become a vital part of our armed forces.

Before there was a national capital, the Constitution gave Congress the authority to set aside a track of land for the purpose of becoming the seat for our national government. The actual site for the seat came about during the Washington administration as a form of compromise between the North and the South. The South conceded certain advantages to the North and the Capital was placed in the South. If you study a map you can see that the capital was placed about midpoint between the states as they existed at that time. Back then, when travel was at a snail's pace compared to what it is today, the location of the capital was extremely important, especially for those in southernmost Georgia and northernmost Massachusetts. Sometimes, state capitals and county seats were placed by having two riders at opposite ends of the populated areas ride toward a given direction, at a given time, on a given day. At the location where the two would meet, there the seat of government would be placed - thus insuring an equal distance between both extreme locations. Many county seats were placed at such locations so that a circuit judge could ride from county courthouse to county courthouse in one day's ride. This prevented him from having to sleep the night, out in the "Holiday Inn" of those days; the cold, wet sod.

Section 8 of Article I ends with a little segment known today as the Elastic Clause. It states that Congress has the power to make any law necessary for the purpose of carrying out those duties mentioned in Article I. Along with the Interstate Commerce Clause, this Elastic Clause aids in giving Congress more power than was expressed within the Constitution. It is nicknamed the Elastic Clause because it can stretch the Constitution to give Congress a lot more power if needed. It takes into account the unforseen situations that the framers could not visualize at the time of the writing.

SECTION 9 POWERS DENIED TO CONGRESS

Our Founding Fathers, or at least some of them, wanted something to be put into the Constitution which would state in black and white what Congress could not do. The section is similar to most of the amendments in the Bill of Rights in that it is written up as the negatives or the "cannots" of Congress.

As was previously stated, the issue over slavery was a very hot item to discuss, and the attitude prevailed that "the less said about it the better." The first clause in Section 9 states that the importation of slaves will continue for 20 more years until 1808 at which time Congress would determine whether to continue the slave trade or not. Congress could impose a tax on the importation of slaves of not more then $10.00. In 1808 the slave trade was abolished by act of Congress and the $10.00 tax was never imposed. It took a great Civil War to really settle the issue of slavery in the United States.

The Constitution says that our privilege to a writ of habeas corpus shall not be suspended. This writ is a court order requiring that a person be brought before a judge and the reason for his incarceration be explained. It is hard for most of us to believe that in many places in the world, a person can be thrown into a cell by a whim of an official, and be literally forgotten. A person could remain in jail for a long time without it being determined as to whether or not he actually should be there. This clause usually brings to my mind the story of the Count of Monte-Cristo about a man who was thrown into a dungeon and forgotten. He would have stayed there until he died had he not escaped.

Congress shall pass no Bills of Attainder of Ex Post Facto Laws. A Bill of Attainder would be a law passed to punish one person. An Ex Post Facto Law would be a law that punishes a person for committing an act that was not against the law at the time it was committed.

Clause 4 is a provision that has been made null and void by the passing of Amendment 6 which was ratified in 1913. Originally this clause stated that Congress could not impose a direct tax upon the people of the United States unless divided evenly among the states population-wise. Our 16th Amendment commonly referred to as our "Income Tax Amendment," changed all that. The "whys and wherefores" will be further explored when we come to that Amendment.

No taxes shall be imposed on goods that are exported from the states. Congress must be fair. They cannot make laws concerning trade and commerce that would favor one or more states over others. The states cannot place tariffs on interstate trade. Remember, this was done by states under the Articles of Confederation and it really messed up the country.

Money cannot be taken from the Treasury of the United States without an act of Congress. This is another of our Constitutional *Checks and Balances*. The President is held in check in his power by the simple fact that Congress controls the purse strings of the United States Treasury. He must beg Congress for money and usually makes it known publicly, as to how much he will need during his State of the Union Address. When he finally submits his budget, he usually gets less then he asks so he would be wise to ask for more than he knows he will get.

No titles of nobility can be given by Congress. We really cannot relate to this clause and never give it much thought. However, this was important to the authors of the Constitution. In most countries at that time there were men of noble significance walking about. The "Lords," "Sirs,"

"Your Excellencies" were very prevalent and because we had just fought a war against a nation where those noble titles abounded, a reaction on the part of Americans not to have those titles was evident. After the French Revolution the reaction against the nobility was evident in the title of "Citizen" that was pridefully bestowed on all the people. When the Russian Revolution took place, "Tovarish" or "Comrade" became the title associated with citizens of the USSR. In France and Russia it was a verbal declaration that now all the people are equal. In a few cases when "titled" immigrants had become citizens of the United States, they had to drop their titles of nobility.

SECTION 10 POWERS DENIED THE STATES

The states tried to act like independent nations when America lived under the Articles of Confederation and it did not work. Our founding fathers decided to make it impossible for the states to negotiate separate treaties and to coin their own money. The states were also denied some of the same powers that the federal government were forbidden, such as ex post facto laws, granting titles of nobility and making laws to breach contracts.

The states shall not tax imports or exports, but can make laws governing inspections. Any profit from such fees will be turned over to the federal government.

The states shall not keep an army and navy in times of peace, make treaties with another state or nation, or engage in war unless invaded or if the state is in such danger that it cannot delay action.

This is the conclusion of Article I of the United States Constitution. It is the longest article within the document and the powers are more specified here than in the other Articles. It is the scope of the Legislative Branch (lawmaking body) of the federal government. It laid the foundation for all the laws that were enacted, both good and bad, over the last 200 years.

CHAPTER 7 THE EXECUTIVE BRANCH

ARTICLE II THE PRESIDENT OF THE UNITED STATES

It has already been stated that a long hard war had been fought to get rid of a ruler (King George III) and it was a very difficult task to try to get the colonies to agree on an executive officer - or a man in charge. It was also stated that our first government under the Articles of Confederation did not provide for a one-man executive. Instead they had a committee of lawmakers whose job it was to run the business of government while congress was not in session. To put it in the most simple terms; the people were scared to death of a ruler and were reluctant to create one.

Common sense got the better of the framers of the Constitution. They knew that an executive officer was needed and they provided for one in Article II, but it becomes evident by reading this article that the executive officer, who was chosen to be the President of the United States, was given very little power. His main task was to execute the laws passed by Congress. He also was given emergency powers - those vital powers that must be vested in one man, such as planning a war and making a decision that had to be made immediately. An example of those powers, which were obviously unable to be expeditiously carried out by a congress or a committee, would be: Suppose the U.S. was in the process of being invaded and action against that invasion had to be spontaneously dealt with. Imagine what damage could be done if the country had to wait for Congress to convene and for all the discussions to be heard and finally a compromise and a vote taken for action? The gears of democratic process grind slowly.

An important question could be asked at this time. If the Constitution limited the powers of a president, why is it that the presidents of today are so powerful? When George Washington was unanimously elected president it was as though he went into an empty office. He put some of his ideas into it and as the 200 years of our history went by, all the presidents going into that office brought in some of their own ideas. Today, we have the office of the presidency pretty filled up. Sometimes acts of Congress and Supreme Court decisions take some of the ideas out.

George Washington had a very difficult job in that he had no other president before him whose examples he could follow. Furthermore, with everything he did, he would set an example (precedent) for all the other presidents that followed. It is easier to meet a situation by following the course of action of a previous executive than to prescribe action of one's own creation. It seems that Americans will not resent a presidential order as much if it follows the course of action set by another.

Throughout the many years of our existence many presidents met crises by prescribing an entirely new course of action. Others came into that office following the precedents of those who came before them and also establishing precedents of their own. What we have today is a conglomeration of precedents established by many presidents. It sounds rather impressive to say that the office of the President of the United States today is "the sum total of the personalities of ALL the presidents that have held that office in the past 200 years." More will be said about precedents as we go along.

SECTION I THE PRESIDENT AND VICE PRESIDENT

Section 1 states that the executive power shall be given to a President and he, along with a vice president, shall hold that office for a term of four years. It should be noted that there is no reference to the number of terms that would be allowed. This will be discussed in Amendment 22.

This section shows the fear that some framers had for the common people. They felt that the people lacked proper information and could be easily misled by any charlatan or demagogue that would happen along. They put the responsibility of voting for a president into the hands of electors chosen by the state governments. The amount of electors that a state would have depended upon the total amount of senators and representatives of that state. The states would decide how the electors would be chosen. However this clause states that federal lawmakers and federal office holders cannot become electors.

Clause 3 describes, in very belabored detail, the procedures used by the "Electoral College" in electing a president. This clause is "history" now because it was changed by the 12th Amendment and the development of political parties. The election between Thomas Jefferson and Aaron Burr and the confusion that it created, helped to bring about the 12th Amendment. In essence, this clause said that each elector would vote for two candidates. The candidate receiving the majority would become the president and the one who came in second in the polls became vice president. A problem with this procedure was that the president and vice president often were political rivals and some were not exactly the best of friends. One point of Article 2, Section 3 and the 12th Amendment was that out of the two candidates that the electors could choose, one could not be a resident of that elector's state. This held a limit to the "favorite son" idea because one can see the obvious tendency on the part of states to want to choose candidates from their own states. Today, elections are held in the states to choose "groups" of electors who are pledged to a particular candidate. The popular vote determines what group will cast their ballots. The electors vote in December after the general election. All the votes from the group must be cast for the same candidate - votes are never split. The framers did not anticipate the influence that political parties would play in the election of presidents. This caused an interesting development in U.S. History. More of it will be discussed later.

Congress was given the power to set a time for the election of presidents. In 1792 they chose the first Tuesday following the first Monday in November. This is a fancy way of saying that if Tuesday falls on the first day of the Month of November, the election would be held off for another week.

The Constitutional qualifications for this great office are very few and simple. The candidate must be a natural born citizen. One little line in clause 5 states that he had to be a citizen at the time of the adoption of the Constitution because the nation was obviously so young that almost everybody at that time was not born a citizen of the United States. (There was no United States of America when most of the men qualified to run were born.) This line no longer applies after 200 plus years.

A candidate is required to be a resident of the United States at least 14 years prior to running for office, thus preventing a person from living overseas and being influenced by "foreign" concepts and then coming back to become president. There was also a concern of possible secret allegiance that a person could develop toward another country. In many cases presidents were overseas before the 14 years was expended, however that was in connection with working for the United States government. An example was Eisenhower because he was commander of the armies in Europe prior to his becoming president.

It is required that a presidential hopeful be 35 years of age. The discussion over who was the youngest president is interesting. John Kennedy was the youngest elected president but Teddy Roosevelt was the youngest to hold the job because he came into office as a vice president replacing the assassinated McKinley.

Even though the Constitutional requirements for a president are minimal, in order to become a president a person must be highly qualified and he must work hard and have many achievements under his belt. It has already been stated that there are several "roads" a person can take to achieve the presidency. One is through the Legislature. A person must become well known for popular achievements. He has to be in favorable public limelight. Another very sure road to the presidency is to become a hero general during a war. After almost every major war, we have had an ex general president. We didn't have one after World War I, but that wasn't because we didn't try. General "Blackjack" Pershing flatly refused the job. We didn't have a general to become president after the Spanish American War but we did have Teddy Roosevelt who was a hero in the famous charge up San Juan Hill in Cuba. However he was a vice president who got his presidency as a result of the death of McKinley. Another road to the presidency is through the governor's route. The people will accept an ex governor if great attention is given to his achievements in that office. It is helpful if a man was a governor of a large state. More than likely he would carry his state and have many electoral votes in his favor during his election. A great many presidents were lawyers, but we have had engineers, teachers, college professors, a peanut grower and a haberdasher.

In pursuing the line of the social requirements for the president, we have established the fact that a presidential hopeful must get the favorable eye of the public. We have had a few "dark horse candidates" who have been successful but the reason for their success seemed that the public voted against some other candidate that was too controversial. Traditionally, a successful candidate had to be male and white, have good appearance, (I had a sister who voted for Ike because, as a result of her immense political expertise, she felt that he was "cute."), be popular, and have a good "American name," unless his achievements were such that the name didn't make any difference. An example would be Eisenhower. A hopeful had to be Protestant - until J.F.K. got on the scene. When Catholic Al Smith ran for president, the scare tactics that the opposition used in some areas of the country, were to inform the public that the Pope had his navy standing off our shores, ready to come in and take over should Al win. (This brings to mind the fears that the founding fathers had about allowing common, uninformed people to participate too extensively in government: "The people want for information and are easily misled." One audience was very shocked to learn that a certain presidential candidate had actually "matriculated" while he was at college. For shame!) Getting back to the point made about appearance, I have heard it said and I don't know how true it was, that one reason Thomas Dewey lost the election was because he wore a mustache in the time that it was unfashionable to wear one. (The villains wore the mustaches in the cinema of the 1940's - not too many good guys had them - and of course the greatest villain of that time, Adolph Hitler, sported one.)

Because, traditionally, the people were not necessarily motivated to vote over issues, the personality of the candidate became the order of the day. Great expense was utilized to bring across the personality of the candidate. The "selling" of a president in modern times, is in the hands of the Madison Avenue types who go to great pain to find what the American public wants in a president during a campaign, and will fashion the candidate in such a way as to comply with the image necessary to please the public. This seems deceitful, but the public, being bombarded every day by the advertising on TV, has become conditioned to this type of procedure and in the political world: "If it ain't broke - don't fix it."

This idea of shaping the image of the man is not a new thing. In the election of 1840 great pains were taken to break down the influential image that Jackson projected upon the office of president. Before him, all presidents were well educated "aristocratic type" men. Jackson came on the scene much to the chagrin of the well to do "proper" people in the east. He was a frontiersman, an unpolished Indian fighter without a formal education. (He actually was more polished than his image projected.) Jackson's popularity among the more common people, who were slowly beginning to vote and participate in our gradually developing democracy, had to be dealt with. His two terms of office were up and he was not seeking a third term but his influence in the Democratic Party was still something with which to be reckoned. The Whig party, to identify with the newly franchised common people, came forward with a campaign that would put envy in the eyes of today's Madison Avenue set. They created a logo to grace the Whig party - a log cabin with a keg of cider next to it. This became the log cabin in which Whig candidate William Henry Harrison supposedly was born. The cider jug in the logo was suppose to be the jug from which Harrison "faithfully and excessively" drank. In this case the Whigs turned around a small amount of negative press, put out by the Democrats, to their advantage. The logo was a bonanza to the Whig party, because the common man could relate to all this. The truth of the matter was that W. H. Harrison was born rich, in a large house no way resembling the log cabin that helped him to become president.

To further influence the public to go "Whig," a huge ball was constructed and was pushed through several states to create political fanfare. Thus the expression: "Let's get the ball rolling," came into existence. "Get on the bandwagon," became another time honored slogan that goes back to those political times when bands actually did get on wagons and were pulled along the country-side playing music, to get the attention of prospective voters.

In order to counteract Jackson's influence, the Whigs had to look around for a hero general because Jackson had distinguished himself as the general who whipped the British at New Orleans during the war of 1812. That battle was fought after the war was over, but it didn't make any difference to the American public.

However antiquated he was, General William Henry Harrison was that man. The country was running out of its supply of hero generals and they had to select him even though he was in his seventies. Harrison was a hero of the Indians Wars and he whipped Chief Tecumsah's Indians at the Battle of Tippecanoe many years before.

Because John Tyler was running as vice president on the Whig ticket, the pre Madison Avenue planners came forth with the catching motto of the Whig party for 1840: "Tippecanoe and Tyler Too!" Some say that it was the first of the modern "hoop-la-laden" campaigns. It is interesting to note that Harrison did win the election but died a month after his inauguration. He took his oath of office on a cold and damp day and paid the price for it. He became sick soon after.

It should also be noted that as our developing democratic process advanced to a stage where more common people got the right to vote, the election campaigns became more and more flamboyant and ostentatious to arouse the interest of those people.

We spent many years on constitutional shaky grounds when it concerned the succession of power to the vice president. All the Constitution said on that matter was: *In case of the removal of the President from office, or his death, resignation, or inability to discharge the powers and duties of the said office, the vice president takes over.* The "inability to hold office" was the part that could cause the problem. What constituted the term "inability" and who shall be responsible in determining this inability? During the 19th and most of the 20th century, the only time that vice presidents succeeded to the office was, conveniently, through the death of a president. There were no two ways about being dead. No one had to determine the degree of "deadness" and no one needed to determine whether the president in fact was actually dead or not. What was expressed in Clause 6, under these circumstances, was adequate.

When Wilson was felled by his stroke, he laid in bed unable to do very much, as the country waited for the little time left in his term of office to expire. He definitely was unable to carry out his duties as president and no one took any steps in the process of replacing him. No one really knew the method to use, consequently the vice president did not take over. It has been said that Wilson's wife ran the country until his term ran out. She looked after Wilson and determined who his visitors would be.

When Eisenhower was president, he had a serious heart attack and Vice President Nixon was put in as acting president until that time arrived when Ike was able to once again take over the helm. Fortunately, Ike was in control of his mental facilities and was able to delegate this authority.

It was upon the shooting of JFK that the inadequacies of the Constitution in providing a method for determining how a president could be removed from office, was brought to light. Kennedy lived for about one-half hour, as I remember, and the question was brought up, "What if he would have lived in a vegetative state? Who would have the authority to determine whether he should be removed and how would it be accomplished Constitutionally?" With this unanswered Constitutional shortcoming in the public awareness - made possible by the Kennedy assassination and the situation involving Eisenhower's sickness, it was not long after that the twenty-fifth Amendment was brought into existence.

There was little problem over constitutional interpretation when the first death of a president took place. It was mentioned earlier that William H. Harrison died after only one month in office. The bigger problem was: what role should John Tyler play in the replacement of that president? Some felt that he should simply carry out presidential duties and stay in his role as vice president and not even live in the White House. Tyler established one of those precedents that was discussed earlier, by demanding that he become the President with no holds barred.

If a president was blessed enough to survive his tenure, the office of vice president was not an exciting job until recently. Jokes were told of the obscurity to which that job condemned political hopefuls. Vice presidents did not get to be president when they ran for that office on their own merits during the last and well into this century. An anecdote was prevalent about the vice presidency; "A women had two sons. One went off to the darkest jungles of Africa as a missionary and the other became the vice president of the United States. Neither son was heard from again." The conservative Republicans put Teddy Roosevelt on the ticket with William McKinley because they feared his progressive tendencies - this was a sure method of exiling him to political "never, never land." Their ploy backfired upon the assassination of McKinley.

A President's salary shall not be increased or decreased during his term of office. He shall not have any other source of income from the United States government. He does have a couple of expense accounts and has many fringe benefits including free rent, an airplane, "limo" service and retirement benefits. Considering his awesome job and his likewise responsibilities he does not get all that much pay when his salary is compared with that of the major corporate executives. There is a feeling on the part of many people that it would not be a good idea if we were to elect a president who is after the job just for the money. Many feel that a man should be successful in life before he becomes president. After all, how can we gauge a man's potential success in the White House other than looking into his past to ascertain the success that he has had in other areas of endeavor. Many have actually lost money when they became president. U.S. Grant holds up the bottom of our "successful presidents." He was a failure in every business venture that he endeavored. He rose to great heights for one brief period in his life - as the hero Northern general of the Civil War. As president he was a failure as he was in his other enterprises.

Before a person can become president, he must take an oath of office. That oath is: "*I do solemnly swear (or affirm) that I will faithfully execute the office of the President of the United States, and to the best of my ability, preserve, protect, and defend the Constitution of the United States.*" When Washington concluded his oath of office he added "So help me God." Because of this, he established a precedent. Consequently, all other presidents have added this phrase. This added comment gives a very good illustration of the "precedent factor" mentioned earlier in discussing Article I. The Chief Justice of the Supreme Court administers this oath of office.

SECTION 2 THE POWERS OF THE PRESIDENT

He is the commander-in-chief of the Armed Forces and the Militia when it gets called into active duty. The clause actually said Army and Navy but the assumption is it would include any branch that could be developed as time passed. Someday in the future, the president will command the Space Force of the United States if it comes to that. The military is therefore under the command of a civilian. This is a good thing because sometimes the mentality of a military man is such that he may not understand all the ramifications of a conflict in which his country may be embroiled. Being a civilian, the president is entitled to seek the advice of military men. Our government has a military Chief of Staff that heads the advisory group comprised of officers of all the military units. He advises the president on all military matters.

During the Civil War, President Lincoln had a problem. He had no dependable military men from which to get advise. Until Grant came along, Lincoln was up that proverbial creek without his paddle. He began researching military books in order to develop some expertise in that department. His military service was limited to a few armed skirmishes with Indians when he was much younger. Gen. McClellan was supposedly the big man but Lincoln didn't have much faith in his ability as a military advisor.

At the beginning of the war, it was supposed that Lee would become the big general of the Union, but when Virginia seceded from the Union, Lee felt that he owed his allegiance to his state more than he did the federal government. The feeling of nationalism that had begun to rise just after the War of 1812, had begun to falter and the concept of sectionalism had begun to develop in the attitudes of most Americans.

Grant began to gain a reputation with his victories in the West and Lincoln began to feel that Grant was the man he needed. Grant had a reputation of over indulging in alcoholic beverages earlier in his life and that label was still forced on him. Lincoln was warned to that effect. "Find out what he is drinking so that I can give the same to my other generals," was Lincoln's remark to that warning.

During the Korean War, Eisenhower was elected president because many people felt that it would be very reassuring, during this period in history, to have a tried and proven, honest to goodness military man as our commander-in-chief of the armed forces. His statement, "If I am elected, I will go to Korea," put goose bumps on many an epidermis. To think that this commander of the Allied Armies in Europe during World War II, who whipped the Germans, would actually go to Korea and see for himself what had to be done. This promise was awe inspiring to say the least.

Clause 1 also states that the president has the power to grant pardons and reprieves, except in the case of an impeachment. Through the years many presidents have utilized this power to grant pardons. Lincoln's sensitivity was evident in the fact that he pardoned young Union soldiers from the death penalty because of their inability to cope with their military responsibilities during the Civil War.

Clause 2 declares that the president can make treaties with foreign nations and can appoint federal judges and other federal officers with a two-third consent of the Senate. This is another prime example of the checks and balance system of which our Constitution abounds.

After World War I, President Wilson went to Versailles, France to participate in the peace treaty to settle that war. Wilson was an idealist who had studied the reason for wars. He condensed all the reasons for all the wars in history to thirteen causes. Onto these thirteen causes for wars he added a suggestion to form a League of Nations. He took these fourteen points with him to the peace conference, assured that the rest of the leaders would be seeking desperately for a solution to the many, many wars that were constantly being fought in Europe. This highly idealistic president, like a lamb before wolves, came face to face with the leaders of the other allied nations - which was to come face to face with the hard core reality of European politics itself. They tore his 14 points apart as they tore apart Germany and the Austrio-Hungarian Empire. They did, however, accept his fourteenth point and formed a League of Nations.

The Senate, because the Allied leaders rejected Wilson's proposal for peace, felt so repulsed that they, in turn, rejected the idea of joining in this newly formed League of Nations. Wilson felt that this was a grave mistake and began to plead his case to the American public. He went by train throughout the country giving whistle stop speeches from the back of the train - as was the custom in those days. His trip was drastically halted when he was felled by a very serious stroke. This had a devastating effect on world history.

Some historians say that one reason for the outbreak of World War II was the absence of the influence of the United States from the League of Nations. Another reason for World War II was the hatred that became a part of the German mentality as a result of their feeling of betrayal by the Treaty of Versailles. An armistice ended World War I, not a surrender. An armistice is an agreement by both sides to stop fighting until an acceptable treaty can be worked out. The leaders of Great Britain and France mostly, chopped up Germany and took most everything away from them - supposedly their ability to make war. Later Hitler constantly made reference to Germany's betrayal at the hands of the Allies during the Treaty of Versailles, as he conditioned the German people to accept his leadership. The "if" in history is a very elusive thing. What *if* the Allies had accepted Wilson's fourteen points for peace? What *if* the Senate had approved our entry into the League of Nations? What *if* Wilson had not been felled by his stroke and had been successful in convincing the American public to put pressure on their senators to approve our entering into the League of Nations? The answer to these "if's" - we will never know.

The president has the power to place people into vacancies created while the Senate is in recess. These commissions will expire at the end of the next Congressional session.

SECTION 3 PRESIDENTIAL DUTIES

The president shall from time to time inform the Congress of the State of the Union. At first this was done through writing, but the practice changed to an actual address by the president to a joint session of Congress. This is done in the House chamber because of its ability to accommodate more people. The president talks to a packed house. Besides both Houses of Congress, the Supreme Court is there, the president's cabinet, his chiefs of staff, and his advisors. His family, friends, and many visitors are packed in the gallery.

The assumption is that the president is the most informed person in the United States (not the smartest.) At his fingertips he has access to a network of information and intelligence that is mind boggling. With just a phone call he could put into action thousands of people all over the world working overtime and burning the midnight oil to compile a report on any subject that it is humanly possible to gather. Sometimes the mistakes that a president makes can be traced to misinformation that was compiled for him. In this case it is the president who must take the blame. This was evident with Kennedy's "Bay of Pigs" fiasco. Harry Truman's remark about the buck stopping at the president's office is very accurate.

With this access of information, the president must inform Congress about the condition of the country. Since these State of the Union messages have been broadcasted for several decades, the event has become an instrument used by presidents to appeal not only to Congress for programs and money needed, but directly to the American public.

Presidents can call a special session of Congress in case of emergencies. After the bombing of Pearl Harbor, a special session was called by Franklin Roosevelt to get Congress to declare war on Japan. They did this one day after the bombing. You will see, many times over, on television, that momentous "Day of Infamy" speech given by Roosevelt. A president can, if ever a situation is deemed necessary, adjourn either House until a more appropriate time.

A president is also the "Head of State." He shall receive ambassadors and other public ministers and be present at all types of functions. Protocol mandates that the president shall meet with a ruler, monarch, prime minister or representative of another country, if at all possible. The story is told about a certain foreign dignitary who called upon Thomas Jefferson at the president's mansion. (It was not called the White House at that time.) Jefferson who was most unlike any of the other preceding presidents and not a stickler for formality, met the man at the door instead of a servant. Jefferson was very informally dressed and had to convince the foreign dignitary that he was actually the President of the United States. This was so unusual in the world at that time that the man was highly insulted by Jefferson's actions. This is the same Jefferson who walked to his own inauguration and could be seen, many times, horseback riding about the capital city unescorted.

The president shall see that all the laws are properly executed. This is his big job. The executive branch of our government employs more people than any of the other branches. Through the president's cabinet, newly enacted laws become the responsibility of the various departments in which the law falls. For instance: If a law was passed to increase the rate of a postage stamp, that law would become the responsibility of the Post Office Department. The hundreds of post offices and the thousands of employees of that department would assume the responsibility of putting that law into reality. Stamps are printed and much public information is given about the increase and the date that it will be put into effect. If a law is passed concerning foreign relations the same would be done through the State Department. Not only will orders go down through the ranks in those various departments but information, in the form of reports, will begin to filter up to the top - including the president if he needs it. Of course the president presides over his cabinet and the ultimate responsibility lies with him.

SECTION 4 IMPEACHMENT AND REMOVAL FROM OFFICE

This section, short and simply, states that the president and vice president and all civil officers can be subject to impeachment for treason, bribery or other crimes and misdemeanors.

A common misconception that I have run across as a teacher of the Constitution has been the idea that impeachment meant the actual removal from office. If a man has been removed from office the proper expression is that "he has been impeached and removed from office." Impeachment means the legal proceedings; including the charges brought against the official by the House of Representatives and the subsequent trial that is held in the Senate. Whether or not the man is removed depends upon the way that the Senate votes.

Andrew Johnson was the only president that was impeached but he was saved from removal by one vote in the Senate. It was not that he was a bad president, he was the wrong man in that office at the wrong time. It was after the Civil War and he was a Southerner by birth and he, like Lincoln, tried to bring the South back into the Union without much retribution. The Radical Republicans in Congress wanted the South to be more "reconstructed" before it was allowed back into the Union. It is the opinion of some historians that Johnson stood in the way of those Congressmen in power. Rumors have circulated for decades, around the historical pot bellied stove, about the conspiracy on the part of some government officials to have Lincoln assassinated because of his very lenient policy toward the defeated South. These are only conjectures and have no basis in reality.

Nixon was very close to impeachment and decided to take the path of least resistance and removed himself from office. It would have been an interesting trial.

That is all there is of Article II, the Executive Branch. Keep in mind the power that has increased for the presidents through the years. We have had powerful presidents and weak presidents. It seems that during times of need, our society will seek out the right man for the job. This last statement can be open to discussion. Does the right man for the job coincidently come along at the proper time in history or does the times shape the man? Does our society elect the proper man for a certain era in history? There were times that we have had weak presidents at the time that our country did not want too much interference. During the 1920's, when everything was going fine, people wanted the federal government to keep hands off the affairs of the nation and the presidents who were picked did just that. Of course when the depression hit, President Hoover and the Republicans were blamed for doing the job that the people wanted them to do - to keep hands off.

One more concept of government should be mentioned. The president is the representative of all the people. President Jackson greatly developed this concept. Members of Congress have their own local constituents for whom to fight and these constituencies can be embroiled in their own regional concerns and conflicts. Sometimes it is the president who must have the interests of all the people and the nation at heart.

CHAPTER 8 THE JUDICIAL BRANCH

ARTICLE III THE SUPREME COURT
Sections 1, 2, and 3

SECTION 1 FEDERAL COURTS

The Supreme Court is vested with the judicial power of the United States. Lesser (inferior) courts will be established by the Congress. Judges of both type courts shall hold their position for life as long as they conduct themselves properly. They will be paid for their work and their salary shall not diminish during their continuance in office. The judges are therefore free from any pressure of a cut in pay when they perform their duties. The fact is, the only thing they have to fear is impeachment or dying of old age. The framers wanted to have one branch of government whose members were entirely free from the pressures of having to answer to the people, especially free from the pressures of reelections. There was and will be times in American History where the desire of the people may not be what is entirely good for the country. Human nature, being what it is, reflects that, most of the time, individuals desire what is most pleasing to them immediately, without regard for the future. Many cannot envision the consequences of a present course of action. Government official who are subject to elections are mostly motivated by the desire to please their constituents, so that they have opportunity for reelection. Some presidents and members of Congress lost their popularity by being moved by conscience to do those things that they thought to be right, but were not satisfactory to the people. Other presidents were popular by doing those things to please the people at the moment but have caused bad consequences for the future. Can you image the future of a law maker from a tobacco growing state who introduces a bill to abolish cigarette smoking because he feels that in the future many lives will be saved? Some Supreme Court Justices have been very unpopular with many Americans through the years, however they go about their business of Judicial reviewing unaffected by opinion polls.

SECTION 2 JURISDICTION OF FEDERAL COURTS

Here is a brief listing of the types of cases that the Federal Courts has jurisdiction over: *All cases of law and equity under the Constitution, the laws of the United States, treaties made or about to be made, all cases effecting ambassadors and other public ministers, all admiralty and maritime cases, cases concerning controversies to which the United States may be a party, to controversies between two or more states,* (This underlined clause was deleted by the eleventh amendment.), *between citizens of the same state claiming lands under grants of different states, and between a state or the citizen thereof, and foreign states, citizens, or subjects.*

This clause defines those cases over which the Supreme Court has Original Jurisdiction. That is to say those cases that come initially to the Supreme Court without beginning in a lesser federal court. Those cases include matters effecting: ambassadors and other public ministers, cases in which states may be a party. In all other cases the Supreme Court will have Appellate Jurisdiction - that is to say, the case must start in the lesser courts and possibly work its way to the Supreme Court. There is an exception to all this if Congress makes one.

Trials of all crimes, except in cases of impeachment, shall be by jury; and such trials will be held in the state where the crime was committed.

If the crime was not committed in any state - perhaps out at sea - then Congress will decide where the trial will be held. (Amendment Six of the Bill of Rights further elaborates on jury trials.) In this clause we can see a statement that was a reaction to the pre Revolutionary British activity of sending Americans accused of crimes, mainly smuggling, back to England to stand trial. The colonists were very upset over this. Once they burned a ship that was scheduled to take a prisoner back to England. The reasoning behind the statement that a trial should be held in the location where the crime was committed, was the simple fact that the accused would be near his friends and supporters to help him in his trial. The accused, sent 3000 thousand miles away would have none of these benefits. People did not travel as much at the time this document was written and in most cases crimes were committed in the locale where the accuse lived. Today we have a more mobile society and this is not always true. Travel is not the problem that it was 200 years ago - expense of travel and not the time involved, seems to be the biggest problem of travel in modern times. We see many cases on TV where a family will visit an accused thousands of miles in some remote corner of the world.

In a situation where a defendant feels that he will not have a fair trial near the scene of the crime, he can petition the court for a change of venue (a change of location) for the trial.

SECTION 3 TREASON

The definition for treason and the label of traitor has been a very arbitrary thing throughout world history. These definitions and labels were used as a convenience on the part of rulers to dispatch unpopular adversaries in an expedient manner. A traitor was one who "displeasured" the king. Treason was going against the wishes of a king. The framers of this document were all too familiar with the labels and accusations thrown around by the British in pre Revolutionary days, and they wanted treason to be spelled out so that this label could not be used as a convenience for removing unpopular ideas and inconvenient adversaries.

The Constitution defines treason only as levying war against the United States or helping an enemy wage war against the United States. It is very difficult to convict a person for treason because this section also states that: *no person shall be convicted of treason unless by the testimony of two witnesses to the overt act, or on confession in open court.* Usually, because of the difficulty of convicting someone for treason the defendants are tried for a crime known as espionage. It carries a lesser sentence but it is easier to get a conviction. During the 1950's a famous trial for treason was against Julius and Ethel Rosenburg who were found guilty of passing along the secret of the atom bomb to the Russians. They died in 1953 in the gas chamber amidst much clamor and protest by some Americans.

Congress can determine the punishment for treason. In past civilizations, an accusation of treason carried the same penalty to the entire family of the accused. In different cultures, in different eras of history, the entire family, immediate and extended, and all assets could be done away with. In Nazi Germany, checks were put on acts of treason by the fear that the entire family could be eliminated or their property confiscated. Field Marshall Rommel who was a hero to the Germans was implicated in the plot to assassinate Hitler. Because of his popularity he was given a choice; commit suicide and be buried as a German hero or be tried as a traitor and have his family suffer the consequences of being the family members of a traitor. Naturally he chose the former of the two and killed himself. Because of many movies depicting the intimidating nature of the Nazis toward innocent relatives, an expression that was used extensively in years past that was reminiscent of the threat that the Germans placed on people, even outside of Germany, was the fact that they had control of people's extended family in Germany and would cause them to be put in fear for their lives if a certain person being threatened did not comply with what the Germans wanted. That expression was: (Of course done in the classic German accent) "You have relatives in Germany?" It is very important therefore that, this second clause of section three, includes a statement that only the individual will suffer the punishment for treason - neither his family, nor his property can be touched.

There was once a movie about Israel under Roman conquest - about the time of Christ. A Jewish family was watching a parade from the roof of their home. A tile broke loose at a most inopportune time and landed amidst the parading high Roman officials. The noise of the tile crashing on the road caused the horses to panic consequently, one Roman official unceremoniously spilled on the ground. As punishment for this "act of treason." the members of the household were rounded up and their house and possessions confiscated, the male member of the household was enslaved on a Roman galley ship and his mother and sister were thrown into a dungeon where they subsequently contacted leprosy. Obviously, they had no Constitution to safeguard their rights.

This is the extent of the constitutional explanation of Article III, the Supreme Court. The biggest power that the Supreme Court has is not written in Article III, and that is: it has the power to interpret the laws as to whether or not they are constitutional or unconstitutional. This power was brought about through the setting of precedence by the judges. They took the "bull by the horns," so to speak, and established this power. The Supreme Court under then Chief Justice John Marshall took on a case involving a man who was promised a government position. The man did not get his job and he sued; stating that he had the right to the job under the Judiciary Act. The Supreme Court's decision was not along the lines as to whether the man was entitled to the job or not, but was based on the fact that the Judiciary Act was unconstitutional. In this *Marbury vs. Madison* Supreme Court Decision of 1803, the power of judicial review was established for the courts by the Supreme Court itself.

Some say the Supreme Court is the most powerful of the three branches of our government. A law enacted by Congress can be overturned by the court system. (If that law is challenged.) The actions of the president can be curtailed by the courts or legislation. The only way that a Supreme Court Decision can be overturned is by a Supreme Court Decision to the contrary, or by an amendment to the Constitution.

When the Supreme Court ruled recently that a federal law forbidding flag burning was unconstitutional, those Senators and House members, who were upset over this decision, immediately began to push for a Constitutional Amendment to override the Supreme Court decision that allowed flag burning under the First Amendment. The idea suffered the fate of most of the amendment proposals in history - it died.

CHAPTER 9

ARTICLE IV RELATIONSHIPS
Sections 1, 2, 3 and 4

The states have, throughout our many years under the Constitution, developed into such a relationship with one another and with the federal government, that it is hard to imagine that there was a time in our history when this relationship did not exist. It must be remembered that when this document was written, these relationships had to be created out of the clear blue sky and put down on paper. This relationship that we are now experiencing is a tribute to the genius of our founding fathers.

SECTION 1 OFFICIAL RECORDS AND ACTS

Each state must recognize the official records and judicial acts of any other state. Congress can pass laws to bring this about. The following are some examples: If two people are married in one state they must be recognized as married in any state in which they care to reside - the same is so with divorce. A birth certificate or drivers license from one state must be honored in all other states, but a person must adhere to the driving laws of the state which is being visited. If a person becomes a resident of another state, he will be required to get a license from that state.

SECTION 2 PRIVILEGES OF CITIZENS

A citizen of one state shall be a citizen of any state in which he cares to reside and shall have all the privileges entitled him. Clause 1 allows us to move about freely from state to state to live and work. We are offered the same privileges as those who have lived in that state all their lives.

This second clause of Section 2 sets forth the process of extradition - that is to say that a man who commits a crime in one state and flees into another state shall upon demand of the governor of the state from which he fled, be brought back to that state having jurisdiction over that crime. A governor does not necessarily have to return a fugitive if he feels that justice would not be served in bringing the person back. Lawyers will, most of the time, get their clients to "waive extradition." That is to say, they will get their clients to voluntarily go back to the state where the crime was committed. This eliminates the formal extradition procedure. In a sense, the waiving of extradition will show a little cooperation on the part of the person in custody and every little thing counts when it becomes time for sentencing.

South Carolina delegates at the Convention felt that fugitive slaves should be returned under Clause 2, as were common criminals. They were unsuccessful in bringing this about. Clause 3 was added to cover runaway slaves, however, the clause was ambiguous in its nature and later the process of returning runaway slaves was better defined in the Fugitive Slave Law of 1793.

Fugitive slaves and indentured servants who escape and flee to another state can be held and returned to their owners. This third clause in Section 2 and subsequent fugitive slave laws (1793 and 1850) were nullified by the post Civil War Thirteenth Amendment which states that there will be no more involuntary servitude in the United States. After the Constitution was drafted, this clause gave Congress the right to pass the Fugitive Slave Law (1793) which set forth procedures for returning runaway slaves to their masters. One flaw existed in all this which infuriated the Southern slave owner - the North did not fully obey these laws. Escaping slaves had to get across the Ohio River in the West or over the Mason Dixon line between Maryland and Pennsylvania in the East and they were free in all intent and purpose. Northern law officers would simply refuse to return these slaves as required by the Fugitive Slave laws.

When California wanted to come into the Union the question arose as to how it would enter in - as a slave or free state. This was a crucial matter because California's statehood would upset the delicate balance that was then in existence in that there were just as many Slave States as Free States. This balance was helping to hold things together. Even though tempers flared between the North and South, there still was a type of harmony in the federal government, because any law that was passed had to get through the U.S. Senate. There was an equal amount of Northern and Southern Senators to make sure that both sides were relatively happy with a law before it was passed. The South was so angry over the lack of support on the part of Northerners for the Fugitive Slave Laws that they gladly conceded to allow California to come into the Union as a free state. The concession on the part of the North would be to have the government strengthen the Fugitive Slave Laws thus compelling the authorities in the Northern States to return the South's runaway slaves. This event in history was known as the Compromise of 1850. Slaves who ran away after this compromise had to make it to Canada in order to be free.

SECTION 3 NEW STATES AND TERRITORIES

New states may be admitted by the Congress into this Union. New States entering the Union shall have all the rights and privileges of the older States. The admission of states into the Union has been a vital and interesting part of our history. We started as thirteen states and have worked our way up to fifty. No new state can be made from a part of a state or parts of other states without the permission of those states involved and the federal government.

West Virginia falls into the category of originating from a portion of another state. When Virginia seceded from the Union following the opening shots of the Civil War, Virginians living in the Western part of that state did not want to secede. They formed their own state and remained loyal to the United States; entering the Union on June 20, 1863 as the 35th State.

At the very beginning it was planned that as a state entered the Union, a star and a stripe would be added to old glory. This procedure was done for a while. By the War of 1812, our flag had fifteen stars and fifteen stripes representing the number of states in the Union at that time. Many are aware that the poem, "The Star Spangled Banner." was written by Francis Scott Keye during the battle of Fort MacHenry during that war. The flag that was waving while the "rockets were 'red glaring,' and the bombs bursting in air," was of the fifteen star and fifteen stripe variety. This flag hangs in the Smithsonian in Washington D.C. Some felt that stripe adding would eventually produce a flag with so many stripes that the stripes would not be distinguishable at a distance and the flag would not look too good, design wise, as pale pink.

Congress can set up laws to govern and dispose of territories or other property of the United States. Many movies and tv shows have been made concerning the people in the territories of the Old West. The gun slinging United States Marshals of the old western territories have become a legendary part of Americana.

SECTION 4 GUARANTEES TO THE STATES

The federal government will guarantee the people within every state, a republican form of government (where officials are elected by the people), and protect each of the states against invasion. An invasion of a state would be an invasion of the United States and upon agreement of the state, either the legislature or the president (when Congress cannot be convened) will offer protection against domestic violence. In essence, this is what the Constitution is all about. This simple clause in section 4, Article IV is part of the covenant made between the government and its people. In chapter 4, when the nature of a constitution was defined, one definition given was that a constitution was a contract between a government and its citizens. The people consent to obey the laws of the United States. For this obedience, the above mentioned are the guarantees that the government of the United States offers on behalf of the people. In other words, a state and its people shall be secure in its republican form of government and will never have to fear a takeover by a subversive group or a foreign country.

Nothing, nor no one may deprive the people of a state from having a state constitution that is compatible with the Federal Constitution. The thought of any of the preceding situations happening are not even in the priorities of awareness in the minds of the American people. It is inconceivable that these events could happen, however, two things must be asked: Do we not think of these events happening to the states because they are by nature unable to happen or is it the fact that we have a safeguard to keep them from happening? Hindsight allows us to pass these things off lightly, but during the framing of the Constitution, things such as these last mentioned possibilities, were of foremost concern in the minds of the framers of this document.

CHAPTER 10

ARTICLE V AMENDING THE CONSTITUTION

The framers realized that in order for their document to last through the ages, it would have to be made flexible enough to bend with the stress of changing times. Ships are made in such way that they are able to bend somewhat in rough seas. The Empire State Building sways in high winds. Palm trees weather hurricanes nicely. All these successes are due to the fact that they all bend with stress. This is true with constitutions; if they are to last they are to be capable of bending with the currents of changing times and as is true with glass, if it is rendered brittle and incapable of bending, it will surely break with little provocation. Article V was designed with change in mind. Rational people realize that society changes as it goes along - sometimes not always for the better.

Article V sets up several methods by which amendments could be added, if they were ever needed. The framers set up an alternative method for amending this document, just in case a situation presented itself whereby the government tried to prevent the people from adding a much needed amendment. More will be explained when we approach these methods in this article.

It is not an easy task to bring about constitutional change. An amendment can be proposed by a two-thirds vote of both Houses. An amendment can also begin upon the application of the law-making bodies of two-thirds of the states to have the U.S. Congress call a national convention. (This second choice has never been used.) Here is a double safeguard for our protection. Theoretically speaking, an amendment can begin either by the Federal Government or by the State governments themselves. One thing that should be grasped from this study of the Constitution is the fact that they had designed within this document many checks and balances and safeguards. It seemed that the framers were cautiously aware that an executive, the law-makers or someone could possibly go bad and they had incorporated within this document many methods by which to circumvent a possible corrupt person or branch. No better is this shown then in Article V.

All the aforementioned was for a proposal for an amendment only. That which comes next is for the ratification of the proposal. Three-fourths of the state legislatures must approve of the proposal or three-fourths of the conventions held in the states must approve. The Congress of the United States must determine which method should be used. It is no easy matter getting changes in the Constitution by amendment. An amendment involves more effort on the part of more individuals and state governments. It is a tribute to the planning on the part of the original framers and a realization of the difficulty involved in amending, to be aware that we have had only twenty six amendments to the Constitution in over two hundred years.

ARTICLE VI SOME MORE PROVISIONS

There were several provisions left over at the Constitutional Convention that had to be placed somewhere in the Constitution so Article VI became a catch-all for these provisions.

Section 1 Payment of Debts. This section is a confirmation that the new government would pay the debts that were incurred under the Articles of Confederation. So many countries that have changed their governments because of revolutions make it plain that the new government will not be held responsible for the debts of the government that was disposed. At the time of our Constitution's birth our government was in great debt (so what else is new?) to foreign nations and to the American people who had loaned money toward the war effort. One of the unsuccessful facets of the first government under the Articles of Confederation was the inability to pay off those war debts.

The receipts that the people had from the government were beginning to be looked upon as worthless scraps of paper. Speculators were buying up this paper for practically nothing with the hopes that someday the government would pay off. When our first Secretary of the Treasury, Alexander Hamilton, in order to establish our monetary responsibility, began to redeem these notes, the American people who had already sold their notes to the speculators, were enraged and felt that a deal was made by Hamilton to inform those speculators as to his intent. They felt as though the speculators with, this information, went out and bought up as many of these "scraps of paper" as they could at a small fraction of their value. There is no historical fact to support those allegations of conspiracy.

It should be well noted here that our change of government did not have the ingredients of a fairy tale where, after the Constitution was installed, that everybody "lived happily ever after." Never in our history have we ever been put into a situation where we could lean back and say that all of our problems were solved. Like the history of an individual, the history of our country is a series of solving one set of problems after another. Even before we solve the problems that we have, new ones are formulating for us to work on, they in turn eventually blossom into fruition.

Section 2 puts the status of the Constitution in black and white for everyone to plainly see. The Constitution of the United States shall be the supreme law of the land. There is nothing hidden between the lines or loop holes to circumvent this meaning.

The first serious challenge to this concept of Constitutional superiority came very early in our history. Not long after our new government got underway, the Alien and Sedition Acts were passed by Congress. These laws were enacted because the Federalists believed too many people were criticizing officials in government. A lot of criticism came from non-citizens so the Alien Act made it more difficult for a foreigner to become a citizen. Meanwhile the Sedition Act made it possible for citizens to be fined or imprisoned for criticizing the government. This was a blatant violation of the first amendment and Vice President Jefferson, who could not turn to the federal courts because they were Federalist controlled, called upon the states to pass laws challenging the supremacy of the U.S. Constitution. (I might add here that these Alien and Sedition Acts were looked upon with disfavor and were part of the reason why the Federalist Party began to fade from the American scene.) Because they were introduced by those states for which they were named, the Kentucky and Virginia Resolutions brought forth a doctrine claiming that a state can judge for itself the constitutionality of a law. Other states did not agree, so these resolutions were left unchallenged. The Alien and Sedition Acts were never enforced and were done away with when Jefferson became president in 1801, but the question over Constitutional supremacy vs. states rights was to be a topic that would be discussed at dinner tables and in parlors for many years to come.

When tariffs began to be beneficial to the North and started to hurt the South (the South called it the "Tariff of Abomination"), the controversy over the supremacy of the Constitution reared its ugly head again. Calhoun, a spokesman for the South, espoused the idea of a state being able to declare an unjust federal law, null and void. This process was call "Nullification." The problem over slavery further strained the controversy.

All this bickering was speculative until the final proof of the supremacy of the U.S. Constitution over the states came, as a result of the Civil War. This war answered the question once and for all. In modern times even though the Constitution was somewhat challenged during the Civil Rights movement of the 1950's and 60's, the question has been put to rest. The Constitution IS the supreme law of the land.

Section 3 This section makes it necessary for anyone taking a job with the federal government or the state governments to take an oath of office. However worded, it must state that the person affirms to uphold the Constitution of the United States.

This section further states that no religious test shall be required as a qualification for any government position. The framers were cognizant of the negative aspect of religious bigotry at the time when the United States were still English Colonies. At that time, many countries in Western Europe and elsewhere were still strongly entrenched in national religions, and it was a little rough to belong to a minority religion, sect or denomination within those countries. The framers knew their history and were well aware of the religious persecution that had brought some of their forefathers to these shores. This is the reason for this clause being placed within Article VI. A lot more will be said about religion when we get to the First Amendment.

In essence, this is the extent of the United States Constitution as it is applied to us today. The seventh and last article was put into existence to accomplish one certain task. Once that task was completed, it really doesn't effect us today. We will find out what Article 7 accomplished in the next chapter.

CHAPTER 11 ACCEPTING THE CONSTITUTION

ARTICLE VII RATIFICATION

The ratification of the convention of nine states shall be sufficient for the establishment of the Constitution between the states so ratifying the same.

Between the years 1787 and 1789 each state held a special convention for the purpose of determining whether or not the Constitution should be ratified (accepted.) With hindsight available to us, it is difficult to understand why Americans were against the Constitution. Debates were the order of the day during those years. Even men that we today consider great Americans, spoke out bitterly against this document. They did not have the test of time to draw from in shaping their opinions.

Fear for what some felt was too strong a government, and a government that could go bad after a while, were the reasons for this anti sentiment - pure and simple. Many felt that the document put too much power into the hands of the federal government, especially Congress. "These monied men, these learned men," debated one American describing the convention delegates, "would wish to swallow up us little folk as the great Leviathan swallowed up Jonah." Patrick Henry and James Mason of Virginia and Governor Clinton of New York were a few of many great American patriots who opposed this Constitution.

During these years of debate, the Federalists, those who advocated the new Constitution, began to write essays bringing forth the merits of this document. These writings were compiled and history knows them as the Federalists Papers. Slowly, an idea began to filter in concerning a compromise. It wasn't an entirely new idea because it had been around for a long time in English Law. The idea said in effect; "Let us incorporate into this Constitution a set of amendments - a Bill of Rights." This Bill of Rights would be written in such a way as to disallow Congress to make laws on certain matters concerning individual freedom. If one looks at the sections of Article I, he can see that they are written in such a way that a person could possibly become concerned about individual freedom. What he would see is stated as: Congress can, Congress shall, Congress will. It is obvious that the people back then, freshly separated from a strong government (Great Britain) and not being able to prognosticate the future, would be a little hesitant with all these "cans, shalls and wills." These newly incorporated Bill of Rights would be written in a negative way - that is say: Congress cannot, shall not, shall never, et cetera.

In order for the Constitution to become the law of the land, the Federalists agreed to incorporate this Bill of Rights and slowly the state conventions began to swing around in favor of the Constitution. The promise was made that upon the construction of the government and during the first session of Congress, the Bill of Rights would be created, voted upon and amended into the Constitution. State after state began to sign until, finally, the number of states that were needed in order for this document to become the law of the land, had finally ratified.

WHAT KIND OF GOVERNMENT DID WE GET?

Another issue that was fought over during the Constitutional Convention was the type of government we should construct. Should we have a national government that would be responsible to the American people directly, or should we have a federal government that would be responsible to the state governments? In the latter, the state government would in turn be responsible to the people within the state - as were the states under the Articles of Confederation? Some felt that the government to be formed should follow the pattern of the government set up under the Articles of Confederation, only more powerful. Of course, others argued against this idea and preferred a government that would involve itself with the people directly. As a result of all this, a central government was created that was both national and federal in scope. In other words, it was a national government in that it reached across state lines to involve itself directly with the people of the United States and it was federal in that it was a government involved with the state governments. Direct population involvement was not as great at the beginning but as time went by, the federal government began to become involved more and more with the affairs of the American people. As the state governments failed in certain aspects to satisfy the needs of the people within their states, it was a logical move to look toward the federal government for assistance. Many "states righters" approach this development with dismay and feel that federal governmental control is one step away from freedom as we should know it.

To conclude this part of the Constitution it is necessary to list the types of powers that our Federal Government has and does not have. First are the enumerated powers. These are the powers that are listed in Article I of the Constitution. They are the powers given to the Congress of the United States - such as the power to print money, declare war and so on. Second, there are the denied powers of congress - they are the listed powers that Congress does not have. For example: granting titles of nobility, making ex post facto laws, and passing bills of attainders. Third, there are the reserve powers - those powers that the states never gave to the federal government but kept for themselves. They are the powers that concern the people living within a state and their relationship to the state government. Fourth, there are the concurrent powers - they are the powers that are shared by both the states and the federal government; such as taxation. Fifth, last but not least, are the implied powers of Congress - the powers not mentioned in the Constitution but assumed that Congress must have, in order to do the job mandated by the Constitution.

The Constitution sets up the guidelines upon which statute laws are made. It gives the Congress the right and responsibility to develop laws that fit into the framework of Article I. If a law, created by Congress, is challenged by the people, it will be considered by the Supreme Court or the lesser courts, to ascertain whether or not that law fits within the guidelines. If it doesn't fit, the law then is tossed out as being unconstitutional.
The next chapters will bring us into the third part of the United States Constitution - the Bill of Rights and the total twenty-six amendments.

CHAPTER 12 THE BILL OF RIGHTS

Remember that Article 5 sets up a procedure for amending the Constitution. We must credit the framers with the good insight to realize that changes would be necessary as time went on.

With the hindsight of 200 years of living under this document, it is very difficult to understand the reluctance on the part of many great and well meaning Americans to accept this new framework of government at the time of its inception. Their awareness that governments have gone and could go bad and the still fresh memory of unfavorable experiences suffered at the hands of mother England, played a vital part in this reluctance.

The delegates finally ratified the Constitution and copies went out to all the states. Conventions were held in each state for the purpose of ratification or rejection. Men debated and made speeches for and against ratification. Speech making seemed to be more of an art in those days than it is today. Oratory was the "in" thing and it is easy to envision these men strutting around choosing their words well and gesticulating in the proper mode of the day. Vocal chords were in good shape because men had to make their voices heard without the aid of electronics. While this was happening, the Federalists had their "papers" which were intending to make the public aware of the merits of the document.

From the signing of the Constitution by the delegates at the convention in 1787 to the final adoption in 1789, the document was up to very intense scrutiny. Fear prevailed that this document was allowing too much power to be vested in a central government. Finally light could be seen at the end of the tunnel when the idea for a Bill of Rights took hold. The Federalists and the pro Constitution faction agreed and the states began to fall into line by adopting the Constitution. The agreement was that when the government was formed and the session of Congress begun, one of the first orders of business would be to add a Bill of Rights in the form of Amendments. This was done and in 1791 the Bill of Rights became part of the Constitution.

In the beginning the Bill of Rights concerned only actions involving the Federal Government. When the fourteenth amendment became a reality after the Civil War, the Supreme Court used the due process clause within this amendment to extend many of the rights to protect people against actions by the states. The states cannot deny in their constitutions those freedoms that have been given to the people in the United States Constitution.

AMENDMENT 1 OUR FREEDOM OF RELIGION, SPEECH, PRESS, ASSEMBLY, AND PETITION

FREEDOM OF RELIGION

I don't feel that I need to remind the reader of the tremendous influx of colonists that have come to these shores seeking religious freedom. During the 17th century the countries of Europe were locked into a one religion per country mode. A residue of the middle ages was still evident and a great emphasis was placed on religion. It was mentioned in an earlier chapter, that religion could sometimes play a very important part in a government exercising control over its people. Of course during the Middle Ages, Europe was religiously under the control of the Pope. The Pope told kings what or what not to do. This remained true until the protestant reformation. The authority of the Popes began to wane in regard to religious control over kings, but the outcome was a rigid type of control employed by kings over their subjects. Regardless of the religion practiced in a country there was little tolerance for any other spiritual persuasion. Citizens who were led to any other course of spiritual conviction, were not tolerated in many countries. Discrimination took place in many forms: from down right physical abuse, imprisonment, destruction of sites of worship, unavailability of employment, degrading social status and peer rejection. It must be stated that some countries were more tolerant than others. Holland was an example of a country with more toleration.

When the Pilgrims left England to escape religious persecution they first went to Holland to live. Part of the dissatisfaction that they felt for Holland was that, as farmers, they could not adjust and compete as city dwelling artisans with the Dutch - who were working at these trades all their lives, but they were also appalled by the liberal conduct of the Dutch people. These religious Pilgrims could not fathom the frivolity of the Dutch populace. Their complaints were that they danced and made merry and did not keep the Sabbath.

England practiced religious intolerance as did France and Spain. However the situation in England was such that the opportunity to leave was available to those who were unhappy with their status. When the companies received their charters from the King, they needed people who were willing to leave the places where they lived all their lives - people who were willing to uproot themselves and to brave mortal danger and severe hardships, to colonize a distant land, never to see their English homes again. The people who would most likely do these things would be people who were very unhappy with their life situation. Contented people usually like being where they are - they do not wish to change. People led by other religious and spiritual convictions that were contrary to government policy, and frustrated by the restrictions placed upon them, would be very good prospects for recruiting.

Freedom of religion obviously played a very important role in the development of the English colonies. There were people in some of the other countries that wished for religious freedom also but because of the nature of their governments, they were not afforded the opportunity to leave.

Many people of the 17th century, being a product of gross intolerance, took on these same characteristic as part of their psychological make-up. Many of those who fled the shores of England because of the burden of intolerance placed upon them by their government and its citizens, exhibited the same intolerant behavior toward others when they established their colonies in the New World. When the Puritans established their "Kingdom of God on Earth" in Massachusetts, woe be to anyone who maintained a different spiritual conviction from theirs! Some colonies were more liberal in that they allowed anyone who worshipped Christ into their land.

The framers of the Constitution were well aware of the history involving the sought after freedom of religion on the part of their ancestors. They wanted to make it plainly understood that this quest for religious freedom would be made available.

The interpretation of religious freedom, as with the interpretation of our freedom of speech, is a hot item of today. How far can this religious freedom be carried? If you harbor the conviction of human sacrifice in your religious ceremonies, would this constitutional freedom allow you to participate in such a ritual? This seems a little bizarre so let us settle upon a more moderate problem. Can a person who is of a religious conviction that medicines or a blood transfusion are not allowed, refrain from having them administered to him at a hospital? Another example; Suppose parents try to keep those medical aids from their dying child? These are matters that have been presented in our society and it boils down to the fact that the courts must decide on the basis of constitutionality. An issue that has been foremost in the minds of Americans has been the recent elimination of prayer in public schools because of violation of religious freedom.

Our freedom of religion is a precious commodity and should always be guarded. The very nature of religion is such that when it becomes a part of the spiritual conviction of a person or group, it is a very strong motivator indeed. Wars have been fought in the name of religion. Sometimes both warring parties have prayed to the same God for victory. Some groups have felt absolutely convinced that what they believed was the "true religion" and have either coerced others to embrace that religion or have persecuted those who would not. Keep in mind the Puritan's "Kingdom of God on Earth." and the Inquisition of the Middle Ages with the torture chambers.

The Puritans fell into that mold of religious zealots. They set up a theocratic type governmental structure in Massachusetts (a church ruled secular government) that was absolutely intolerant of the convictions of others. Offshoot colonies began, such as Connecticut and Rhode Island, by those citizens of Massachusetts who were forced to leave that colony for criticizing, or not adhering to, Puritan beliefs. One was a Puritan minister who got in trouble with the power structure.

Relics of the Inquisition of the middle ages, practiced as a result of deep seated religious convictions and intolerance, still exist in museums today. The torture chambers, the racks, boot, thumbscrews and the more subtle artifacts for pain infliction, are a grim reminder of the extent that religious conviction played in those days. The concept that the flesh was of no consequence compared to the soul was a driving force behind the activity of torturing a "wayward" person to either confess his sins, or to come back to the "fold" before he died - which in many cases was very soon - so that his soul would go to heaven instead of going in the other direction. Those inquisitors were absolutely, without a doubt, one hundred percent sure that what they were doing was right. They did these things while praying to Almighty God for guidance and praying that God would accept the soul of that "unrighteous, sinful person," who was lying before them; screaming, squirming and causing such a fuss.

I have mentioned the extreme of what had and could happen to a society not covered by religious freedom to make a point. We must guard against those who would want to gain control of our minds and souls.

CHAPTER 13 OUR FREEDOMS OF RELIGION, SPEECH PRESS, ASSEMBLY AND PETITION

FREEDOM OF SPEECH

"Give me the liberty to know, to utter, and to argue freely according to conscience, above all liberties." (John Milton, 1608 - 1674)

The ultimate affirmation to our freedom of speech is embodied in the expression that was attributed to Voltaire: "I disapprove of what you say, but I will defend to the death your right to say it." That expression looks good on paper but very difficult to put into the harsh world of reality. The following scenario is probably more attributable to the nature of the human race: A man is speaking in an auditorium to a group of people and is advocating everyone's right to freedom of speech. He speaks; "I feel that everyone has the right to freedom of speech." A member of the audience stands up and argues, "I think you are wrong, not everyone should have the right to freedom of speech!" The speaker is provoked upon hearing this contradiction and asks security to remove the man from the premises.

Human nature being what it is, the result is clear that this freedom of speech provision in the Constitution can become a very emotion provoking commodity. In principal, everyone feels that it is one of our God given, most sacred gifts. Now everything would be fine if everyone exercising their freedom of speech, spoke only those things with which everyone else could agree. When adversity enters into the picture, and when a person hears things that are disagreeable, repulsive, or go against the very fiber of his moral code, this is where the problem occurs.

On the other side of the coin, it is imperative that freedom of speech should go hand in hand with the little known, long forgotten, concept known as "responsibility." In the "me" oriented society of today, people are using and abusing this precious freedom of speech gift for their own pursuit of happiness or for monetary gain with little regard for the consequences that it holds for others or for society as a whole. When confronted with their "wrongdoing" they begin to hold the Constitution up high and denounce their adversaries with blatant violation of their Constitutional rights.

Legally, there are restrictions to our freedom of speech. The courts try to determine whether a person's freedom to speak interferes with the rights of others. For instance, a person is not utilizing his freedom of speech if he yells "fire!" when there is no fire, in a crowded auditorium, resulting in death and injury to many panic stricken individuals rushing to escape.

Slanderous remarks may end up in court with the perpetrator compensating a person for whom the slander was intended. Our freedom of speech is not extended to a situation whereby a person's words inflame and influence an audience to go home, get their guns and pitchforks and to cause a riot, or move to overthrow the government.

Legally and morally, the precious right to free speech, along with many of the other rights should stop dead when they begin to interfere with the rights of another. This is what freedom and responsibility are all about.

FREEDOM OF THE PRESS

Freedom of speech and freedom of the press are tightly interwoven. The latter is an extension of the former. It has been said that freedom of the mind is paramount to all other freedoms. If the right to gather information and to form conclusions on that information is taken away from a group of people, all other freedoms will be taken away as a consequence. When revolutions take place in modern times, one of the basic strategies is to seize and gain control of the news media. When that goal is accomplished, the people effected by that revolution can be brought into line by being told exactly what the victors want them to hear.

Hitler was a leader to fully realize the importance of the relatively new mass media instrument of the 1930's, known as radio. He mobilized an entire nation into one thought by deliberate mind control, employed through mass communications. His regime became masters at it. They proved that if a people were cut off from all other sources of information, then a massive propaganda strategy could be planned and implemented in order to bring into existence, total control of those people. Under these circumstance, the biggest lie would be believed if told enough times. "Truth" to Lenin and the Communists was anything that would enhance the Communist Party. "Peace" to the Communists was that which would come when the world was united under communism. The communist newspaper, *Pravda,* means "Truth" in Russian. It has probably not always lived up to its name so far as the Western meaning of the word is concerned. Communist ideology has mellowed lately. Things are changing in the Soviet Union with Glosnos (openness). Once put into effect, that country will never be the same again.

Propaganda is that which is used to produce a desired response. It could be the truth or it could be a bold faced lie - whichever produces the desired effect for those in leadership.

We have not been completely devoid of our share of government mental manoeuvering. During World War II our government, through the mass media, made great strides to get the people mentally conditioned to weather an all out conflict. Effort was made to persuade the people to "hate" the enemy and to make all kinds of sacrifices for the war effort. A tremendous feeling of nationalism was issued forth. The flag burners of today wouldn't have stayed too healthy during the 1940's practicing their unique activity, not while America's sons and daughters were suffering and dying for "old glory."

Not only does propaganda continue to flourish on the American political scene in very subtle dosages, it runs rampant in the advertising world. As the little kiddies watch their TV shows Saturday morning, they are being mentally programed as to what to ask mom and dad to buy them for Christmas or other occasions. The method must work, otherwise the tube would not be loaded with the number of cartoon shows crowding the channels. Of course, this mental conditioning will become a behavioral trait as those children grow. Advertisers realize this and they will make efforts to take advantage of this conditioning through all stages of a TV viewers life. One must take note of automobile ads. Transportation is not only sold - an entirely different way of life is sold. In other words you will be able to emerge from the doldrums of your normal existence and drive into a life of excitement, if you buy the proper automobile - or so the advertisement leads you to believe. The American public is led, like sheep, into determining the styles to be worn, the aftershave to use and the automobile that will change a person's image. A considerable amount of money is spent by advertisers, propagandizing the TV viewers, including myself. Hopefully a large amount of people watching television are aware that not all the statements describing a product is necessarily true. Especially those things said about candidates in paid political announcements.

The best qualified candidate is not always elected for a government position. Sometimes it is the person who spends the most money and conducts the better media campaign who wins. It is disconcerting to see the effect that mass advertising has on the populace. It is absolutely frightening to realize that the same methods of mass media persuasion used in advertising, can be employed by a dictator to bring an entire nation into line. This is not the science fiction of *Brave New World* or *1984,* it is the harsh reality of our planet earth.

The Constitution mentions the news media as the "Press." When the document was written, the newspaper was the only thing available, other then Indian smoke signals, the word of mouth or the personal letter. In this century, mass communications, through electronics, has rapidly grown so large and can reach so many people in such a short time, that it is mind boggling to say the least. News travels at the speed of light and can reach millions in seconds through radio and television. The power of the mass media is a tremendous force, and a constant vigilance on this power is absolutely essential in order to keep a society free. Despots, demagogues and absolute dictators rely on mind control brought about through mass communications, to keep their subjects in line.

A test of our freedom of the press came early in our history - long before we had become free of Great Britain. In 1734, years before our Constitution and Bill of Rights, a newspaper editor by the name of Peter Zenger was arrested for criticizing the colonial governor of New York. The charge was seditious libel. Alexander Hamilton, his attorney, argued that the allegations written in Peter's paper were true and therefore not libelous. The jury found Zenger not guilty. This verdict was considered a major step toward the freedom of the press as we know it.

As with the freedom of speech, our freedom of the press has certain restrictions. It must not provoke an immediate danger of insurrection or riot. The writers within a free press must have the responsibility to write that which is true. As we take advantage of a free press, it is the responsibility of the reader to ascertain the validity of what he reads. Always consider the source as the cliche goes. Know the intent of the writer or the intent of the person about which the writer writes. Naturally a defense attorney will show a much different side of the accused as will the prosecutor. A person will not do himself justice if he does not read both sides of an issue before making up his mind. Our freedom of the press must be watched closely and sometimes fought over, in order for it to remain free. The same is true with our other freedoms.

FREEDOM TO HOLD ASSEMBLIES

Because we live in a free society, it is difficult to look upon some of the freedoms we take so much for granted as not being the natural order of things. They are so much a part of the way things are and have been that they become so commonplace they are not even appreciated or considered.

This holds true with our freedom to assemble. "Big deal!" we may subconsciously say, "why even take into account our right to assemble? It is just the natural order of things." Some governments that wish to control its people will not allow any assembly which is not planned or sanctioned by that government. It should be remembered at this point that the British kept the colonial assemblies from getting together to conduct colonial business in pre Revolutionary times. It could be that this was one of the reasons why many wanted this freedom incorporated into the Bill of Rights. Imagine for one moment the Communist countries of a few years ago allowing an assembly of people that were gathered to criticize communism? In the days of Nazi Germany, people had to sneak around under fear of death to meet in some remote and secret cellar. The meeting could have been in all innocence but the suspicious Gestapo (German Secret Police) would most likely break it up instantly and possibly haul the participants off to "who knows where."

The courts have decided that assemblies could not present a clear and immediate danger to its citizens. That is to say if the direct result of a certain assembly incited the audience to go out and start a revolution or a riot, this would not be allowed. What must be taken into account is the fact that the government must protect its citizens of their lives and property. I have stated a simple rule of thumb earlier that should be applied. A person's rights stop where someone else's rights begin.

When we see controversy between factions on TV or in the newspaper, it is usually over the issue of where the rights of one group ends and the others begin. We are all aware that these rights exist - that isn't the question. The question is, how far do you travel on the toes of one side as opposed to the other side that maintains that their freedom is being cut short. I like to use the battle over pornography as a prime example because it is apparently prevalent in all sections of America. On one side the retailers are up in arms because the "anti porners" are trying to interfere with their first amendment right to free speech. Those opposed are upset because they feel that pornography is eating away at the very fibers of the moral fabric of this country. This is a clear example of each side feeling that their rights are being violated. The retailers maintain that those opposed to this material simply should not buy it. To the anti pornography people, keeping this objectionable material out of their homes and away from their children does not end the matter. They feel that the child goes out into the world and becomes adversely affected by the results of this "lowering of social morality,"

FREEDOM OF PETITION

In actuality, a petition is a declaration of a grievance directed at the people who run a government. More sophisticated definitions could be conjured, but this one is simple, unpretentious and understandable. The power of a petition resides in the number of people one can get to support the cause in question. Thus the more people one can get to sign it, the more it will be considered by a government to whom it is sent - especially if those signatures represent the constituents of an elected official. One person could write up a petition and send it off, but it would probably wind up in the round file by the side of someone's desk. The numbers game must be employed in order to get results. Along with Motherhood and apple pie, this is the American way.

Amendment 1, along with Amendment 5, is probably the most widely publicized amendment within the Bill of Rights. You can read or hear about its use and abuse in the papers and on the tube. It is one of the most important amendments in preserving our rights and freedom. Remember, if it is our right as American to employ these freedoms within the First Amendment for our precious pursuit of happiness, we owe it to others to have within us a sense of responsibility, so as not to abuse these rights at the expense of our fellow citizens. Many will not agree, but the rights of others are as important as our own.

CHAPTER 14

AMENDMENT 2

THE RIGHT TO BEAR ARMS

A well regulated militia, being necessary to the security of a free state, the right of the people to keep and bear arms shall not be infringed.

The wording of this amendment supplies a lot of ammunition to the National Riflemen's Association's armory for their fight against those who would limit the use of firearms in the United States. This controversy provokes as much emotional fervor as the controversies that surround the first amendment. It is difficult to sift through all the facts and come to any satisfactory conclusion. The details we usually gather are from the issues presented by those who are at the emotional ends of this argument - they are the loudest - and, like the issues encompassing the first amendment, we sometimes may be forced to accept either the beliefs of one side or the other. One can see evidence, as with the first amendment that some of the champions of our God given, inalienable rights are thus so, not out of altruistic conviction but for pure and simple financial advantage.

Regardless of what side you take in these matters, try to recognize the intent of some of those who would pass on their reasons for guarding our sacred Constitution as unselfish vigilance. Also keep in mind that, no matter what their intent is, nevertheless, they still have the Constitutional right to fight for their cause - as do their opponents.

The firearm was a product of the industrial revolution. Gun powder can be traced back to China long before the Europeans were fully civilized. It took the industrial revolution to utilize the potential of this powder. It was the firearm that provided one of the edges in world domination, of which I spoke in Chapter 1. The edge in technology, such as the firearm, allowed the countries of Europe to essentially go out and colonize the world. Visualize a group of explorers sailing into a world of less technologically advanced people and showing the potential of a musket to those inhabitants who have never seen such a weapon. Imagine them hearing a sound of thunder, a cloud of smoke and seeing some poor soul dropping dead in his tracks. At times those interlopers were assumed to be gods.

One of the most important possession that a person can have in modern times, other than his house, is probably an automobile. In the early days of our history, however, the firearm was the most prized possession that a man could own. With it he could supply food and protect his family from many dangers. The firearm gave the pioneer the advantage over the native American. It could kill at a longer distance and more efficiently than the conventional bow and arrow. A man in colonial days, especially on the frontier, was never far from his weapon. He coddled it, cleaned it, took very good care of it, and passed it along to his oldest son when he went to his final rest in that "big frontier in the sky."

The traditional spot for a firearm was on pegs right above the fireplace. It rested at a place that was easily accessible and was close to the warmth of the fire to keep it dry and free from rust. It also served as an excellent spot to keep the gunpowder dry. "Keep your powder dry," is an expression that has come down through the ages that had originated during the musket days when a person had to do exactly that in order not to be placed in a very precarious situation.

In the old flintlock musket days, a piece of flint was locked in place into the hammer and when the trigger was pulled, the flint would hit a striker plate and produce a spark. This spark would ignite gun powder in a little metal pocket known as a priming pan. The burning powder would than proceed through a small hole into the actual barrel of the musket which in turn would set off the packed powder. Expanding gasses would propel the lead ball out of the barrel to, hopefully, hit the object aimed at. In many movies and TV shows about colonial times, where scenes were shown of a person firing a musket, one could observe a puff of smoke appearing close to the head of the shooter a fraction of a second before the gun was fired. Sometimes, with misgivings to the shooter, the little puff of smoke appeared but the gun did not fire. The expression, "a flash in the pan," has come down through the ages as another cliche for our repertoire of fancy sayings.

Eli Whitney of "cotton gin" fame was the first in America to use the assembly line approach in the manufacturing of army rifles. Under contract with the government, he set up tools and dies to "mass produce" weapons. He did not need a group of skilled gunsmiths working like crazy to meet his contractual obligations. With the assembly line concept, he could use semi skilled laborers to produce one particular piece of the entire mechanism. The parts were then assembled into weapons by a few skilled gunsmiths. Besides the expediency with which the musket could be assembled, the advantage of this method of manufacturing was in producing many weapons with interchangeable parts. On the battlefield, two partially destroyed muskets could be taken apart and possibly enough of the intact mechanisms could be salvaged to make one complete gun. Henry Ford would apply this principal to another product later in history.

Technology improved the weapon gradually to produce the state of the art weapons of today: rifling, percussion cap, repeating shot and cartridge weapons. One of the inventions that historians have described as necessary in taming the West was the six-shooter. It gave the settler the firepower of six men when compared to the potential of the one shot musket.

The privately owned firearm was an indispensable commodity in American History. When men met as a militia to safeguard their existence from Indian, French or British, it was the privately owned weapon that was used. Although firearms were supplied to the army, the backbone of our fighting capability was the militiaman with his privately owned musket that did the trick.

With the musket held in such high esteem, and the realization of the potential danger for citizens without weapons, against immediate foe or a bad government, it was perfectly natural for the framers of our Constitution to make sure that our right to maintain a militia and for individuals to possess arms, was stated in our Bill of Rights. However, the need for weapons was much more evident in the 18th century than it is today.

As our society progressed through the many years of our existence, the priority of the weapon has been reduced. Indians are no longer about to burn down our homes or scalp our wife and children and most of us patronize the local supermarket for our food. In colonial times almost everything was done by the family - from protection, food gathering, food hunting, animal herding, carpentry, to educating, soap making, "birthin' babies and doctorin.' Today we live in a specialized society. All the aforementioned activities that were done at home by the individual family members have been farmed out to specialists, who in turn have become experts at usually only one of these activities and farm out their own needs to other specialists, et cetera, et cetera.

One of the activities that has been farmed out to specialists is the responsibility to protect. In the modern area of specialization, we entrust our security to a law enforcement body which is more specialized in this than we are. Theoretically, our need to carry weapons has been minimized. We have a situation that must be reckoned with - that was not evident in the days that produced the rationale for our second amendment. The need to carry weapons has been reduced and the swelling of our population makes it very unsafe for people, some of whom have very limited mental and emotional capabilities, to be running around armed to the teeth with weapons. Governments, whose duty it is to protect its citizens, have placed restrictions upon the accessibility of firearms, especially in the large cities. It seems that rural areas and smaller towns have less restrictions. The interpretation of the concealed weapon as being a "no - no" is understandable. Why would a person conceal a weapon unless he is up to no good? If you can prove that you actually have need for a concealed weapon, it is possible that you could be provided with a permit, if certain rigid rules are followed. Many citizens still keep a weapon in their home for protection.

The dark side of our right to possess firearms must be stated along with the advantages. This right has produced grave consequence to children and families in that many tragedies have occurred when inquisitive children have found and played with daddy's "unloaded" firearm. We have had hunting tragedies where legitimate accidents have happened and where accidents have occurred by very incompetent hunters. Worse of all, we have the availability of weapons for the felon who will use these devices for devious activities. Most tragic of all are the mass murderers, who because of mental instability, will use the availability of rapid firing assault weapons to wipe out a multitude of men, women and children in a matter of seconds.

Because of the varied reasons on the dark side of this issue, we have people whose deep concern for the safety of American citizens, drive them to seek limitations on the use of firearms. This desire to limit weapons puts them directly into the gun sights of supporters of the right to have unlimited access to firearms and who are backed by the big daddy gun club of all times, the National Riflemen's Association, who will pour its resources into seeing that the right to our Second Amendment - the right to bear arms - is not infringed. Solutions are not easy, tempers run high in this controversy, the same as those concerned about the first amendment. Hopefully, cooler heads will prevail and practical compromises will be worked out.

CHAPTER 15

AMENDMENT 3 and 4

AMENDMENT 3 NO QUARTERING OF SOLDIERS

No soldiers shall, in time of peace, be quartered in any house, without the consent of the owner; nor in time of war, but in a manner prescribed by law.

This unobtrusive amendment remains in the background of our Bill of Rights. It is about as silent as the first and second amendment is loud. I have never heard it talked about, discussed or argued, and I doubt whether any type of pressure group will spring up to preserve or advance its cause.

At the time of its writing, the memory of pre Revolutionary War days was still sharp and crisp in the minds of the advocates of the third amendment. After the French and Indian War, the marriage between the American Colonies and Great Britain began to deteriorate - as described in Chapter 2. The British Army, long thought of as the protector of the colonies in happier days, began to be looked upon in a different light. These "lobster backs," called so because of the familiar red uniforms denoting the British soldier, were now being depicted as enforcers of British law. Much to the chagrin of the colonial populace, laws that were on the books for years were now being enforced like never before. To add insult to injury, some of the money from the hated taxes, went toward the keeping of British Troops in the Colonies. In other words, the colonists had to pay good money for what they thought were injustices.

One reaction on the part of the British, because of our refusal to pay these taxes, was to order the citizens, in some places where it was deemed necessary, to quarter soldiers in their households. This Quartering Act was part of what the colonists referred to as the Intolerable Acts that Great Britain passed as a punitive reaction to the Boston Tea Party. The fear that was prevalent in regard to this Constitution - that same fear that produced the other amendments within the Bill of Rights - prompted many to remember this transgression on the part of the British, and to see that this violation would never be repeated.

During times of war, when the United States is involved in a life threatening struggle, if it were absolutely necessary, soldiers could be quartered in private homes, but this amendment states it will be done in a manner prescribed by law. Many of my female students had facetiously remarked through the years that they wouldn't mind the quartering of soldiers in their homes as long as they were young and cute. In times of extreme emergencies, if the preservation of the United States depended upon the setting aside of some of our Bill of Rights temporarily, this could be done. During World War II entire hotels were taken over by the military. However, this was done by compensating the owners.

AMENDMENT 4 SEARCHES AND SEIZURES

The right of the people to be secure in their persons, houses, papers, and effects against unreasonable searches and seizures shall not be violated; and no warrants shall issue but upon probable cause, supported by oath or affirmation, and particularly describing the place to be searched, and the persons or things to be seized.

Once again we must return to pre Revolutionary days to fully understand the desire of the colonist to include this amendment in the Bill of Rights.

The American colonist fought against the idea of "taxation without representation" in different ways. Refusal to buy (the boycott) was then and still is a lethal weapon in the art of protest. An adversary can be injured very effectively when hit directly in the cash register. The boycott was used quite successfully in the colonial struggle against England in pre Revolutionary history. As effective as it was, it sometimes proved to be an obvious hardship on the perpetrators. The story goes that coffee became our national drink when the good people of the colonies had to substitute something for their beloved tea - during the infamous tax on tea. Substitution or complete abstinence seemed to be the order of the day, except for one ray of light - smuggling.

Smuggling was an accepted vocation for many colonists. Many fortunes made by certain Americans could be traced back to a lucrative enterprise of smuggling on the part of their forefathers. As explained in the last couple of paragraphs in chapter 1, the sole purpose for a country going through the trouble of developing a colony is for exploitation pure and simple. The reason for having a colony, in other words, is to benefit the mother country. There were very explicit laws stating that the advantage of trade in the American colonies must go to Great Britain. For years these laws were circumvented through the activity of smuggling. Goods were brought in stealthily from other countries and one of the advantages of smuggling was that the hated tax need not be paid.

Remember, during the 18th century, England was so busy fighting France that they had a tendency to overlook the foibles of the colonists in America. The colonist were able to carry out their unlawful practices without much threat of retribution from the British officials, whom in many instances looked the other way and allowed this to happen. It was only after the French and Indian War that England was able to focus its attention on the misdeeds of the colonists. Compare this situation with the example of the young child that is allowed to run wild all his life and suddenly, he becomes subject to rigid discipline? "No way Jose!" All of a sudden, men were being imprisoned for doing things that they were allowed to do for years. Smuggling had run rampant and many houses harbored smuggled contraband.

In order to expedite matters, British officials were issued *Writs of Assistance*. These so called "legal documents" allowed British officials to search houses indiscriminately looking for smuggled goods. These blanket search warrants ran contrary to British law and even back then, they were considered to be in violation of the rights of the colonists.

Under Amendment 4, search and arrest warrants are issued by a judge, only if there is probable cause. To obtain a search warrant, a peace officer must show that it is very likely that the search will produce evidence of a crime. The exact location for the search must be stated and things suspected must be noted. If some other stolen article not mentioned on the warrant is found, it could not be used in court against the accused.

An arrest can be made by police officers without a warrant when they see a person actually committing a crime, or when they have sufficient reason that a person actually committed an offense. The suspect would surely get away if a warrant had to be obtained. A person's body may be searched when he is placed under arrest. This helps to insure the safety of the arresting officers. A judge may issue an arrest warrant which is served by a police officer. The warrant must describe clearly the nature of the charge. Because of their mobile capabilities, automobiles may be searched without a search warrant. Since the 1960's more attention has been given to the protection of persons arrested, specifically because of the *Miranda vs Arizona*, Supreme Court decision and a few other court decisions, which will be discussed later.

Thousands of television shows and movies have used the scene of the policemen knocking on the door of a house. When the man who comes to the door gives his name, the police then produce a warrant, informs the man that he is under arrest and states the reason for the arrest. The same scenario takes place with the search warrant.

Television and the cinema have worked on the emotions of its viewers by developing the scene whereby the hated criminal is allowed to go free because of an illegal search or arrest, thus putting the helpless victim's life in jeopardy because the hideous, merciless felon is free to seek his revenge.

Early in English law, the concept was developed that every man's home was a castle that no force of government should be allowed to invade. As in many of the other freedoms in the Bill of Rights, it seems that the felon has a heyday abusing these freedoms and mocking our system of justice. This is a tragedy of our system. However these laws are for the protection of all the citizens and are held in reserve in case the honest decent individual ever needs them. If they were done away with for the criminal, they would surely go in the same direction for the average, law abiding citizen. This is true - however unfair it may seem.

CHAPTER 16

AMENDMENT 5

THE RIGHTS OF THOSE ACCUSED OF A CRIME

This amendment like Amendment 1 is the one that has been and will be the topic of many shows in the cinema and on television. Great movies have come down to us through the decades using this fifth amendment as its theme. The airways are filled with news, movies, and classic dramas that have designed plots wrapped around this fifth amendment. There are several provisions to this amendment and the best way of handling them is to take them on, one at a time.

No person shall be held to answer for a capital, or otherwise infamous, crime, unless on a presentment or indictment of a grand jury, except in cases arising in the land or naval forces, or in the militia, when in actual service in time of war or public danger.

A capital crime is the one so serious that a person convicted could face execution. An infamous crime could entail a lengthy prison term. These are the more serious transgressions, to say the least, and it shows the concern of those who incorporated this amendment into our Bill of Right for anyone who would wrongfully be accused of these crimes. It takes the responsibility out of the hands of one person to indict someone on a charge that could take away a person's liberty or life. It would eliminate the possibility of officials who were prejudiced, or harbor a dislike for certain individuals, or who were not entirely clear on all the facts involved to consequently render an arbitrary decision that would send an individual wrongfully down the pathway to penal oblivion.

A grand jury, composed of a number of citizens will hear all the facts presented to them and then make a decision as to whether or not the evidence is enough to indict (charge) the individual for the crime. By using this method, a group of peers will do the indicting and not only one official. This jury should not be confused with the jury who hears all the evidence during a jury trial and determines innocence or guilt. Another advantage to the idea of a grand jury is the fact that it would probably be more difficult to convince a group of people to indict the person in question than it would be to convince one person to indict.

Times of war is a different ball game. The clause within this amendment that mentions the members of the armed services being exempt from this procedure of indictment during war time, shows the concern on the part of the framers that war time is special and has its own rules. Remember the Quartering Soldiers amendment states that in wartime the procedure could be different. In the military, a person is subjected to a Court Martial, which is made up of a panel of officers. Some very tough sentences have come down from these panels during war. Desertion or sleeping on watch could be punishable by death, if the accused had endangered the lives of many who depended upon his vigilance during guard duty, for their safety. This made a very severe statement: "thou shall not sleep on guard duty." As mentioned in a previous chapter, President Lincoln, using his Constitutional right as president, pardoned several frightened, confused young Union soldiers from the gallows or firing squad, when they had been condemned to death by Military Court Martials during the Civil War.

nor shall any person be subject for the same offense to be twice put in jeopardy of life or limb:

Some real strong movies have been made using the above clause. These shows capitalized upon the idea that a person can not be tried twice for the same crime. Many times in my teaching of the Constitution, I developed the scenario that has also been the plots of movies - of the person who goes through the entire trial with the audience believing that he is an innocent victim. Finally upon hearing the verdict of innocent, voiced by the foreman of the jury, the elated movie goers settle back into their chairs to give a proverbial sigh of relief. Their minds are blown when the "hero" of the movie stands up and shouts out that he was the murderer and walks out of the courtroom a free man. According to this clause, he cannot be tried again. This produced debate in my classroom and is a wonderful tool for attention getting, however it does not express the true purpose for this double jeopardy clause being included in the Fifth Amendment.

Suppose a person was innocent and a government, in its desire to punish perpetrators of the law took this innocent person to trial. Fortunately, this person was found innocent by the jury. One year later the government gathered more evidence that pointed to this same person. Back to court he goes and is found innocent again of that crime. This could happen again and again. This person would have the fear of a trial hanging over him time and time again; *to be put twice in jeopardy of life or limb*. "Life or limb" was an expression that was a carry over from the middle ages when, as punishment for a crime, a person could have an hand or arm actually cut off. I doubt whether punitive amputation was practiced in the English Colonies. The double jeopardy clause insures the citizens of the United States that such a situation would not happen. As a result of this clause a person has his "day in court." and it is finished.

Here comes the big daddy of them all:

nor shall be compelled, in any criminal case, to be a witness against himself:

This is the most famous clause in all Constitutiondom. Through the years, the television shows and more resent Congressional hearings have familiarized us with the expressions; "I refuse to answer on the grounds that it may tend to incriminate me," "I plead the fifth amendment," or simply: "I plead (take) the fifth," or "I refuse to answer." Sometimes very hostile witnesses subjected to Congressional interrogation have pled the "fifth" to such questions as; "What is your name?" "When were you born?" It was very difficult for me to convey to my students the idea that pleading the fifth amendment was not an admission of guilt. This idea when built on the premise that an "innocent person has nothing to hide," makes it almost impossible not to look upon the pleader as "guilty as sin." I must confess that it is also very difficult for me to view such hearings and look upon a person who pleads the fifth amendment without forming an immediate guilty opinion. I know that this is wrong.

If one would go back to the middle ages or study the police methods of some countries in modern day, one would understand that there still exists, and did exist, situations whereby hapless individuals suspected of crimes have been pressured, threatened, and tortured into confessing to crimes they did not commit. One story goes back to the middle ages of a person who was placed on the infamous rack and stretched for the purpose of obtaining a confession. The pathetic man, in order to escape the excruciating pain inflected upon him by his tormentors, pleaded pitifully, "Oh sirs, please, please tell me the crime for which I am accused, so that I may confess to it!"

In recent times some countries, especially the Communists, used the method of forcing prisoners to sign public confessions under fear of further punishment, promise of freedom or better treatment. This was evident during the Korean and Viet Nam wars with the cruel and inhuman treatment of American prisoners by the enemy.

Our own country has not been devoid of such persuasion. Methods were employed by police of placing people behind bright lights, with hours of interrogation - until the suspect was broken down to the point where he either tripped on his story or finally confessed. The famous, or infamous term was created; "the third degree." Many movies of the 1940's used this expression in the dialogue between cop and crook. This was the name for the forcefully persuasive methods use to make a suspect talk. The rubber hose was employed to beat a suspect and leave few telltale signs on his body. If any bruises or lacerations were noticeable, the reason was that the unfortunate prisoner "fell down the steps."

Suspects have been tricked into giving confessions by various methods so it is quite important that someone who knows the law be present on behalf of the accused. The ruling in the Supreme Court's case, *Miranda vs Arizona (1966)*, puts an extra burden on the law enforcement officer to handle his arrest according to prescribed procedures, otherwise, the man walks. The Miranda card, the little card that the policeman carries somewhere on his person (sometimes in his hat), allows him to properly read the suspect the rights he has - such as being silent if he doesn't want to talk, if he does talk, he should be made aware that what he says will be used against him in a court of law and to remind the suspect of his right to have a lawyer, paid for or free, by his side. The Miranda card not only reminds the suspect of his rights but also reminds the policeman of the responsibility he has in making a correct arrest.

Miranda was a person who confessed to his crimes in an improper manner. When the Supreme Court, issued forth its decision, many "guilty as sin" people were set free on the bases of this decision. Many Americans were infuriated that these criminals were free to walk the streets again. Many who were freed were arrested after a short time for repeating their criminal activity. Priorities must be assessed on this matter. Is it more important that a few criminals be kept in prison or that officials live up to the expectations of the Constitution? One important thing to come out of all this is a more highly educated and qualified police officer. Remember, a day could come when the reader is faced with an arrest and suspicion of committing a serious crime.

I had a friend many years ago that was faced with a situation for which he was glad to have this fifth amendment to protect him. He came home very late one night which resulted in a confrontation with his irritated wife. After a heated argument he put on a pair of shorts and sneakers and decided to ride his bicycle around the streets to get a breath of air and to settle his nerves. What he wasn't aware of was the strange situation that prevailed in the area in which he was riding his bike. There had been a string of break ins and burglaries in that neighborhood. The only description of the offender was that he wore shorts and sneakers and rode a bicycle to the houses which were burglarized. Because of the frequency of the crimes, the cunning on the part of the perpetrator to elude his captors and the fact that there was not much else exciting for the local police department to do in that small town, they were really laying in wait for the next robbery attempt. My friend later explained to me that they came in on him from all directions - lights blinking, sirens wailing, shouts of every description for him to halt, surrender, and throw down his gun (if he had one) - an arsenal of weapons pointed at him. He was manhandled roughly, thrown down, handcuffed and searched. His cries that they had the wrong man and that he was completely innocent fell upon deaf ears in all the excitement. I feel at that moment in time the police would have bet their eye teeth that they had captured the right man. Just suppose a hideous crime was committed minutes before all this happened, or worse still, a law officer would have been shot and killed by the real burglar. We laughed about this later and I kidded and reminded him of this incident for years, but at that time it was not funny and he could thank God that the Constitution puts certain restraints upon law enforcement officers. As in other amendments, irresponsible people and criminals hide behind these freedoms for their own gain and at the expense of the good people of this nation. That is the price we must pay in order for the occasional innocent people who are wrongfully accused, to have the full protection under our Constitution.

nor be deprived of life, liberty and property without due process of law;

The above mentioned things cannot be taken away from a person without a jury trial. It means more than that. From the time they put the cuffs on a person until they slam the penitentiary doors in his face, a prescribed method of conduct must be evident on the part of the law enforcement officers and the court systems. The best example would be a stairway. Each step must be lawfully taken in order for the next step to be obtained. From the reading of the Miranda rights, the proper holding of the prisoner and his appearance before a judge, through his jury trial, due process must be evident. If a good lawyer can prove that a segment of that procedure had been violated, the man walks.

nor shall private property be taken away for public use without just compensation:

It seems that this clause is out of place in this amendment. Maybe the framers of the Bill of Rights really didn't know where it belonged and didn't want to make a separate amendment, so they threw it in the most appropriate place.

If they survey for a new freeway and the least expensive and most practical route is right through your living room, you and your house will have to go somewhere else. The concept behind this is that the road is for the good of many and your devotion to your dwelling only makes you happy. More than likely, if they did reroute their pathway they would encounter another person who would need to be evacuated from his home. It is easier to remove you and your dwelling then to reroute an interstate at the expense and inconvenience of many taxpayers. You and your house will have to go and you will be paid a fair and just price for your property. Precious memories and sentimentality do not play a part in this compensation.

The fifth amendment works hand in glove with Amendment 6. As the accused ascends up the latter of due process of law he inevitably wraps around himself the protective coat of the amendment that will be brought to life in the next chapter.

CHAPTER 17

AMENDMENT 6 RIGHT TO A SPEEDY TRIAL

As we left chapter 16, it was stated that the sixth amendment seemed to be a continuation of the fifth for a person who is arrested and accused of a crime. This sixth amendment comes into play when the indicted person is ready to maintain his innocence in court. It reads:

In all criminal prosecutions, the accused shall enjoy the right to a speedy and public trial,

The idea of a speedy trial is obvious. A person should not be allowed to sit around in a cell for a very long time waiting for that moment in court when he is able to present his defense to a jury of his peers. To wait a long time for a trial was evident in countries in the past and is still apparent in modern times.

The problem in the United States today is the court dockets are filled to the brim with impending trials. If a person is allowed bail, it isn't as bad. He is set free with an obligation to appear in court at a given time. Although he is free, however, he still has the specter of a trial and possible punishment hanging over his head. Those who, because of the seriousness of the crimes, the lack of responsibility, or past records, are denied or cannot make bail, must sweat it out in a jail cell until the day of their trial. This time spent in jail is deducted from the sentence as a result of the trial. To reduce the swelling case load, the art of plea bargaining allows the accused to plead guilty to lesser charges thus saving the time and expense of a jury trial.

These delays in the trial of individuals are contrary to the Sixth Amendment, but it seems that there still are no answers available that would expedite the solution for sagging case loads. If a good defense lawyer can prove that the government is delaying a trial for too long a period of time the charges can be dismissed.

The fact that the Constitution states the trial must be public, prohibits citizens from holding a trial in secret and railroading the accused to a guilty verdict. If the trial is held in public, the chances are better that the trial will be an honest one, because the proceedings will be held in scrutiny by other people.

by an impartial jury of the state and district wherein the crime shall have been committed. which district shall have been previously ascertained by law.

When faced with the prospect of spending time in jail, it is comforting to know that those who have the responsibility to determine a person's guilt or innocence, are people in the same situation of life as the one being tried. They are referred to as "peers." They must find guilt without reasonable doubt. It is reassuring that when a person goes to trial for the crime of robbing a bank that the jury is not made up of a host of bank presidents. The problem in assembling juries is that sometimes it is difficult to get people to respond to their obligation to serve on juries. Those who have jobs and commitments in the work world, will not find it an easy matter to make a financial sacrifice for this important endeavor. It is so easy to cop out of serving - you simply tell the court that you have already made up your mind as to the innocence or guilt of the accused. (Remember, an impartial jury?) I have been informed that the amount of citizens copping out of jury duty is of mammoth proportions. Many complain that our justice system is inadequate and that the guilty are not being convicted for their crimes, etc cetera. At times it is the very people who do the complaining that will find excuses for not serving on a jury when they are called.

As a result of this unwillingness to serve, the courts get many older retired people and unemployed who would gladly serve to fill up their time and their purses. I am not saying that older persons cannot do a good job - I am in the "older person" category myself, but sometimes defense lawyers are not too happy with an overabundance of senior citizens because of a tendency by them of not being able to relate to the younger generation and the problems that cause them to get into trouble.

I had the pleasure of sitting on a jury for an armed robbery trial years ago, and I saw the ploy that the defense attorney used to try to remove a few older people because of the drug related robberies of which the defendant was accused. He purposefully mumbled things to these seniors when he interviewed them. I was much younger at the time and I couldn't hear what he was saying either. After the third or fourth time that the seniors asked the lawyer to repeat what he said, the lawyer would then ask the judge to excuse the potential juror for lack of appropriate hearing.

In ascertaining that the jury would be impartial, the judge addressed the potential jurors of which I was a member and asked whether any of us had any knowledge of or a relationship with any member of the court. I had to raise my hand and was subsequently asked what that relationship was and to whom it was directed. I told the judge that I had taught the assistant State Attorney, (in charge of trying this case for the State of Florida,) in school as a student. At this point the defense attorney became interested in me and asked if my former relationship with the State Attorney would prejudice me in determining my decision on the basis of the evidence given in the courtroom. I told him absolutely not. He seemed satisfied with my answer, smiled and moved on to other things. At this point I could also see the State Attorney looking over in my direction, trying to recognize who I was. Finally he did and gave me an unobtrusive nod. In a lot of cases concerning younger defendants, it is my feeling that defense attorneys like the idea of teachers sitting on the jury. They feel that, because teachers work with these younger people they can more readily sympathize with the conditions that have caused them to go astray and that this could be a factor in determining the outcome of the verdict. Whether or not this is an accurate assumption is debateable.

The second part of this clause - *in the state and district wherein the crime shall have been committed* - shows that the framers of the Constitution were aware of the fact that crimes in an area were committed by people living within that area. As I mentioned before, travel was at a snails pace 200 years ago when this Constitution was constructed. People more or less stayed in the general area where they were born and lived their lives. It may be hard to understand this in the highly mobile society in which we live today. If the trial was held in the area where the crime was committed, the accused would have the advantage of family, friends, and supporters close at hand. On the other side of the coin, those doing the prosecuting would have the advantage of the proximity of the area where the crime was committed. The framers too well remembered the shipping back to England of those colonists who were accused of crimes, to be 3000 miles away from family or any type of support.

and to be informed of the nature and cause of the accusation:

How can one build up a defense for himself if he does not know the nature of the crime of which he is accused? If one were guilty he would know, but not necessarily so with an innocent person. The lawyer of the accused will get a complete copy of the indictment and will begin planning a strategy based on that indictment.

to be confronted with the witnesses against him:

This ties in with the previous clause. An accused has the right to defend himself, so if a person testifies against the accused, the accused, through his lawyer, has opportunity for a rebuttal.

to have compulsory process for obtaining witnesses in his favor:

How many times has the scene been portrayed on TV shows of the defense attorney trying to seek information to prove his client's innocence? The person is reluctant to talk and finally the defense attorney comes forth with the time worn expression, "If you don't give me that information now, I'll be asking you for it in the courtroom." This lawyer has every right to threaten because of this clause. What the lawyer can do is get a subpoena from a judge forcing the witness to testify in the accused behalf. The biggest reason for people not volunteering their testimony is the simple fact that they do not wish to get involved. I like the story of the man seeing the crime committed and his testimony could easily clear the wrongly accused person but he doesn't want to testify because he happened to be at the spot, where he witnessed the crime, with a women other then his wife. Better still, the other women involved just happened to be his employer's wife. No way would he be willing to testify unless forced to do it.

and to have the assistance of counsel for his defense.

The federal government has been required to have a lawyer for the accused if he lacks money to hire one. This came into effect in 1942. The Supreme Court declared in 1962 that states must also provide lawyers for accused persons who cannot afford council.

States have public defenders who are attorneys paid by the state to represent insolvent people. Before the public defenders, some states had regular attorneys that would take gratis cases on a rotating bases.

I have heard it mentioned many times that if a person needs good representation, he should make every effort to pay for it. This is by no means a slur against the competence of the public defenders, but their case loads are so full that they really cannot take the time and effort of which a paid attorney would be capable. In numerous cases, we can see inequities in society of the rich having an advantage over the poor and this is one of the obvious times. If you are rich you can afford the top of the line defense attorney, some work with teams of lawyers and investigators to get you off the hook. If you are not as wealthy, you can mortgage or sell your house and draw out all your savings from the bank for an attorney that will be effective. The cost will, more or less, depend on the seriousness of the crime of which you are accused. Of course you must weigh the cost of a good private lawyer against the time you may have to spend in prison.

The trials that were discussed in this chapter, dealt with those accused of a crime. They involved a government trying to prove the guilt of the accused so that some sort of punishment could take place. There is another type of trial that will be mentioned in the next chapter. Please, read on.

CHAPTER 18

AMENDMENTS 7, 8, 9 and 10

AMENDMENT 7 JURY TRIALS IN CIVIL CASES

In suits at common law, where the value in controversy shall exceed $20.00, the right of trial by jury shall be preserved,

One person has the right to take another to court if what he feels is owed him to be in excess of $20.00. I have never heard of a case that has involved that little amount of money. During the writing of the Constitution, 200 years ago, that was a lot of money - probably compared to hundreds at today's prices. The states have set up small claims courts to handle suits for small amounts of money. The famous Judge Wapner handled what we would determine to be suits for small claims on television. Sometimes claims are so small that lawyers are not retained to handle these cases and the principles involved represent themselves. The difference between this court and the one talked about in amendment six is that the government is not necessarily involved. A crime need not be committed and one person, a company, or a group of people may be suing one person, a company or a group of people.

and no fact tried by a jury shall be otherwise re-examined in any court of the United States than according to the rules of common law:

If an appeals court reviews one of these cases, it cannot reverse the verdict if that court disagrees. It can only look for legal mistakes that caused the case to be unjust.

Common law is the law or customs to which we adhere. These are based upon precedents established by judges over a long period of time. In contrast to civil law which derives from statutory laws already written, common law puts emphasis on the facts of a certain case so as to arrive at a fair conclusion for those involved in that particular trial. Common law evolved as far back as the 12th century and got its name from the fact that these laws represented the "common" customs of the kingdom. Common law became prevalent in those colonies developed by Great Britain and was, consequently, an important consideration for our Constitution.

AMENDMENT 8

NO EXCESSIVE BAIL OR CRUEL PUNISHMENT

Excessive bail shall not be required,

Bail is paid by a person accused of a crime. It is security against the fact that the accused will appear at a certain courtroom, before a certain judge at a certain given time. If the accused fails to do this he could be hunted down and charged with contempt of court and the money that was paid for his freedom, taken from him. There are bail bondsmen who make a living by putting up the money for a bond. For their efforts they usually charge ten percent. If a person skips out and doesn't appear at the appointed time, the bail bondsman can also hunt down the fleeing fugitive.

Movies, TV shows and nightly news constantly depict the accused meeting or not meeting bail. We are touched by those shows depicting the loving parents who mortgage their home, or use their life savings to bail their unfortunate misguided son out of jail, only to have the ungrateful offspring skip town, which results in the parents losing everything.

How many times has the scene appeared of the person lying on the cot behind bars and the jailkeeper appearing, opening the cell door and saying, "O.K., you're free to go, (so and so) has paid your bail."

The Constitution says that the bail must fit the intensity or seriousness of the crime. Those accused can sometimes be freed until their trial, on their own recognizance. That is to say the judge will feel that the person accused, because of his standing in the community and his reputation of reliability, would make it to his trial without the posting of a bond. The seriousness of the crime will also be a factor in this decision.

I sat in a courtroom as a spectator one time during what is known in Florida as first appearances. This is a procedure whereby the judge determines whether the person should be held for an infraction of a law that he had allegedly committed, or for which he was arrested, usually the night before. The judge will also determine and set bail whenever appropriate.

One very frightened young man was led before the bench and the charges were stated and his defense was heard. The judge wanted to make sure that the man knew that he had to appear on a certain date and the man nodded his understanding to those instructions. The judge then wanted him to give an address that was reliable so that the accused could respond to certain notifications that would be sent him. Whenever the judge would inquire as to his permanent address, the nervous young man tried to explain to the judge that he stayed at different places at different times. The judge then would counter as to where the court notices could be sent so that the accused could receive them. The accused would again begin to explain that he stayed in different places at different times. The judge could not receive a commitment from the accused as to where the notices could be sent. Finally in complete frustration and irritation, the judge, in order to simplify the request made to the fidgeting young man, asked, "Where do you keep your tooth brush?"

The young man being frightened to wits end, in all honesty and sincerity, with no hint of being sarcastic or disrespectful, nervously responded, "In the bath room."

The court room broke up with laughter, the judge pushed his chair back from the bench, lifted his arms in a gesture of hopeless futility and pleaded with the court clerk to handle the unsolved portion of that particular first appearance.

The atmosphere drastically changed with the first appearance of the next and final person. There had been a string of murders that had taken place around Volusia County involving a group of men who would mask themselves and enter homes of people living in sparsely populated areas of that county. They robbed, raped and brutally murdered. They had caused fear and concern for quite a while. I remember my wife pleading with me to put extra locks on the doors - which I did without too much hesitation.

A prime suspect in those murders was to make his first appearance. Extra sheriff's deputies came into the courtroom and the spectators were given an option to leave the courtroom or stay. If they stayed, it was made known that all the doors of the courtroom would be secured and no one would be allowed to enter or leave the courtroom until the suspect was taken away.

The man was brought forth in cuffs and leg irons. The judge became very serious and business-like and the tension was as thick as pea soup. The accused presented himself in a very humble manner and it was hard for me to realize that this person could have committed, or participated in all those horrendous murders.

nor excessive fines be imposed, nor cruel and unusual punishment be inflicted.

Imagine a judge saying, "O.K., you ran a red light - twenty years imprisonment," or "Your punishment for theft is to have both of your hands cut off." In all fairness, the punishment, whether fine or imprisonment must fit the crime. There are guide lines that judges use for sentencing so that a type of uniformity exists throughout a state. The judge also bases his sentencing on other factors, such as the reputation of the person, the record that he has, the intent in which the crime was committed and his co-operation with the system after he was apprehended.

Many feel that the punishment that people receive in America is too lenient and that the victims are left to suffer far more than the people who committed the crimes. Many are infuriated by the release of those from jail long before their sentences are served. Some feel that those condemned to death are kept from their fate by too many years of appeals.

On the other hand there are others who think in terms of using the prisons for the purpose of restructuring the convict's criminal mind to more constructive behavior. They also look upon the death sentence as cruel and unusual punishment forbidden by the Constitution. They feel that execution does not deter crime and serves no purpose except to take away from the humanity of a society. They also fortify their argument against the death penalty by showing examples of people being found innocent years after sentencing.

The Supreme Court ruled many years ago that the death penalty was in fact cruel and unusual punishment and was not impartially given; thus declaring it unconstitutional. Years later they reversed that decision and some states began to use the death penalty once again. Whether one is for it or against it, one fact should be realized; there are very few countries in the world that still use the death penalty.

AMENDMENT 9 RIGHTS RESERVED TO THE PEOPLE

The enumeration in the Constitution, of certain rights, shall not be construed to deny or disparage others retained by the people.

As the Bill of Rights were being developed, some felt that the listing of these rights could produce a misinterpretation that other rights would not be guaranteed because they were not placed in the Bill of Rights. Everyone should realize that all rights cannot be listed, so this amendment made it quite clear that there are rights that the people have other then those listed in the Bill of Rights.

AMENDMENT 10 RIGHTS RESERVED TO THE STATES

The powers not delegated to the United States by the Constitution, nor prohibited by the states, are reserved to the states.

As mentioned in a previous chapter, the colonists felt that the Revolutionary War was won, not by a central government but by a group of individual states winning their separate independence through their own efforts. They realized that a joint endeavor was important.

When the framers wrote the Constitution and began to give certain powers to a central government, those powers that the U.S. Government received came from one source, theoretically speaking; the states - who in turn derive these powers from the people. The states had won these powers, so these powers were theirs to give or to keep. It stands for reason then, that those powers not mentioned in the Constitution must therefore still belong to the states because the states never gave them up. Thus we have the rationale behind the last amendment of the Bill of Rights.

This Bill of Rights, when used by an individual to defend himself from the awesome power of a government, will put that individual on the same footing as the government itself and even more so. This becomes evident by the criminals who makes a mockery of our judicial system. As I watch the news, I am often inflamed by seeing criminals go free or given much easier sentences than they deserve. I grieve for the victims of those individuals that laugh at our system.

It is difficult to keep all this in proper perspective and realize that what we have in this wonderful Bill of Rights is a protection waiting for us in case it is ever needed. It should leave us with a very secure feeling, especially when we view the news and see what is done in other places of the world. We may not agree with what others believe or say but we should be appreciative of the fact that they have a right to their opinion. Remember, as soon as the rights of the opposition are taken away, those rights no longer exist for us either, consequently, we return to square one on our game-board of individual rights and freedoms.

CHAPTER 19

AMENDMENTS 11 and 12

As already stated, the first 10 Amendments are known as the Bill of Rights. These amendments applied only to the national government, however, as a result of the 14th amendment, the Supreme Court had ruled that the due process clause of that amendment is carried over to protect citizen from action against the states. This Bill of Rights safeguards fundamental freedoms from exploitation by a government. The concept of this document did not develop with the colonists. It was an existing thing in English law starting with the Magna Charta of which we spoke in an earlier chapter. More development took place with the Petition of Rights and the Declaration of Rights until this idea leaped across the Atlantic into the English Colonies of the New World.

Both Virginia in 1776 and Massachusetts in 1780 placed within their original state constitutions a bill of rights. These two states along with New York and Pennsylvania refused to ratify the Constitution unless a Bill of Rights was incorporated into that document.

A multitude of ideas were submitted, eventually they were narrowed down to twelve and ten of those were adopted in 1791. This admission allowed the states to adopt the Constitution of the United States.

This Bill of Rights was added to the Constitution all at once. As we look over the remaining sixteen amendments there must be an awareness of the fact that they were added one at a time over a period of 200 years. It is interesting to note that our nation's history would roll by unhindered by any amendment for sometimes forty or fifty years - almost a lifetime to someone living in the 19th century - and in a matter of a few years several would be added. Be aware that when several came in over a short expanse of time, it was as a result of either a war, national trauma or change that had taken place in American life through some progressive movement. The study of these amendments is a study of American History itself because the amendments act as a mirrored reflection of the forces acting upon our country.

When plans are drawn for the purpose of building something, it must be realized that these plans conceived in the mind of the designer may not fully operate perfectly once the article is transformed from blueprint to reality. The new mechanism when built must be put through a carefully studied operation in order to ascertain that the reality of the operation coincides with the calculations of the designer. This operation is called by many names. New aircraft are put through a stringent test by a test pilot. Naval vessels go on shakedown cruises. Automobiles are taken to the test tracks. Great effort has to be made to get the "bugs" out of something newly created.

What could be any different with the development of our government? The plans were laid in Articles one, two and three of our Constitution and it would be impossible for the country to run smoothly without getting some of the bugs out once the government was transformed from blueprint to reality.

The North won the Civil War and with the availability of hindsight at our command we can list the many advantages that the North had over the South. "*Gone with the Wind's*" Rhet Butler was challenged to a duel when he tried to explain to the "Southern gentlemen" that their arrogance would not win the war. The Northern States had more going for them than just the South's lack of "cannon factories" that Rhet mentioned. Among the many advantages that the North had, that many do not consider, is the fact that they had a government that was in operation for seventy-two years. The newly formed Confederate government was untried and untested.

Amendments 11 and 12 were testimonials to the fact that our Constitution was created by man and although they deserve our admiration and appreciation for a job that was pretty darn good, there were still a few bugs that had to be removed from the mechanism, once the government started rolling.

AMENDMENT 11 SUITS AGAINST THE STATES (1794)

Article III, Section Two, sets forth the cases over which the Federal Courts would have jurisdiction. In Clause 3 of that section, it mentions that these courts will have jurisdiction over cases involving citizens of one state who sue another state. Amendment 11 takes away this jurisdiction from the Federal Courts. It also excludes people of other countries from bringing suit against a state in a Federal Court. These suits are now being handled by the courts of the states that are being sued.

This amendment came about as a result of a Supreme Court ruling in the "Chisholm vs Georgia Case." Alexander Chisholm, who was a citizen of South Carolina, brought suit against the State of Georgia for an inheritance over which he felt he was entitled. Because it was mandated by the Constitution that such cases were the responsibility of the Federal Courts, the

Supreme Court took this case. Georgia challenged the rights of citizens to sue state governments and challenged the authority of the Supreme Court in handling such cases. The Supreme Court ruled that what was done was Constitutional. As a result of all this, Congress passed the 11th Amendment which removed the jurisdiction of such cases from the Federal Courts. A tug of war was evident between the federal courts and the state governments. The decision of the Supreme Court on the basis of Constitutionality was nullified by an amendment which changed the wording and therefore negated the interpretation. The states won that round.

AMENDMENT 12 HOW PRESIDENTS AND VICE PRESIDENTS ARE ELECTED (1804)

This amendment best illustrates what was mentioned about getting the bugs out of a newly built machine. Unforeseen problems began to arise over the election of presidents and vice presidents. Please, keep in mind that in the first few elections, political parties, however slowly working themselves onto the American scene, did not play as great a part in electing presidents as they do today. The polarization of groups into parties was a natural progression beginning with the controversy between those who wanted a strong federal government; the Federalists, and those who did not; the Anti-Federalists - later to change its name to a more positive sounding: Democratic Republican Party. I might add that this party was the Great Grand Daddy of the Democratic Party of today.

If you remember, the common people did not have too much to do with presidential elections either. The election of presidents were put into the hands of selected people of each state known as electors. It was their responsibility to nominate and eventually elect presidents. Check out Article II, Section 1, Clause 3, the Executive Branch, for the details

When it came to choosing our first president, George Washington, there wasn't too much of a problem. Washington was very popular and was the only unanimously elected president in history. The difficulty came after his two terms were over. Article II, Section 1, Clause 3 stated that the candidate that received the largest number of votes became the next president and the man who received the second largest number of votes became the vice president. This situation could easily create an embarrassment because a man who wanted to be president and came in second, was now pushed into the number two spot, which could be demeaning to him. The vice president could possibly be hostile to the president because of man's inherent jealousy and because of the fact that he could be a political foe from the opposing party. Remember political parties were slowly forming.

A big problem reared its ugly head in the presidential election of 1800. Thomas Jefferson and Aaron Burr were the top runners and they ended up in a tie. Article II, Section 1, Clause 3 also mentioned that in case of a tie the election is decided by a vote of the House of Representatives. Each time the House voted, it also resulted in a tie. The Federalist Party had its power somewhat weakened because of the unpopular Alien and Sedition Laws during John Adams administration. The people also feared them because they believed this party would lead them into war with France. In spite of their failing popularity they still held enough power to render a stalemate in Congress. The vote to resolve this tie was taken 35 times.

Alexander Hamilton, who was Secretary of the Treasury under Washington, was a spokesman for the Federalist Party. Hamilton and Jefferson were both in Washington's cabinet for a while and their different views and arguments over what course this country should follow have become legendary. Fledgling American History students burn the midnight oil reading and differentiating between Jeffersonian and Hamiltonian Democracy. In very simple terms, they were political adversaries.

Some historians say that it was the influence of Hamilton that finally broke the tie and eventually made Jefferson our third president. Why would this professed political opponent of Jefferson help to make him president? The simple reason was; he may not have agreed to what Jefferson believed but he knew Jefferson to be an honest and honorable man. Hamilton believed Aaron Burr to be a scoundrel. However cordial Hamilton and Burr seemed occasionally, they had a running political feud going for some time.

Aaron Burr, because he came in with the second largest amount of votes, became Vice President of the United States as was decreed by Article II, Section 1, Clause 3 of the Constitution. Obviously, the country was not willing to go through this again, thus we have the twelfth Amendment to the Constitution. It did away with Clause 3.

Burr failed to win the Gubernatorial election of New York because of the opposition of Alexander Hamilton. Hamilton and Burr were not the best of friends to say the least, even before these elections. As a leader of the Democratic Republican Party, Burr was put in direct conflict with Hamilton who was a leader of the Federalists Party. Hamilton had spoken out against Burr publicly and privately for years.

Burr finally challenged Hamilton to a duel. Dueling was illegal but was still practiced. Death was not always the ultimate outcome of a duel, usually satisfaction was obtained by one opponent not showing up or "first blood" in sword duels, being manifest on either of the antagonists. At times the opponents would both fire their volleys into the air, shake hands and go home. In other words, satisfaction was not always obtained by the killing of the adversary.

They met on a field in Weehawkin, N.J. on July 11, 1804. How many times have scenes of a dueling field been reconstructed in the cinema? One can visualize the early morning mist rising from the field and the two participants, attended by their seconds and witnesses, standing in grim silence. Back further are the carriages that had brought the parties to this bleak occasion and a doctor nearby ready to ply his trade.

The story as I recall, reenacted graphically, by an old college professor of mine in our classroom, was that Hamilton fired first and missed. The duel could have been resolved by Burr, holding his fire for a few seconds to make Hamilton sweat a little and then firing into the air. Burr would have won and his honor satisfied, but that would not have pleased him. He had his enemy at his mercy and had all the time he needed, because Hamilton was honor bound to stand his ground. With the smoking dueling pistol by his side, Hamilton awaited his opponents pleasure, Burr took steady and deliberate aim and fired. Burr mortally wounded Hamilton, and was discredited for what he had done. (I might add here that this event may not have happened exactly as stated, but it was interesting to me as I remember my college prof vividly narrating the duel and I know it will make for interesting reading.) Burr eventually resumed his role as vice president. Later he was to be tried for treason because of uncertain land dealings he had conspired in the West. He was acquitted in 1807. Imagine, this man was very close to becoming one of our presidents.

In this twelfth amendment, the big change was that the vice president would be picked on a separate ballot. The electors from each state still could pick two nominees to run for president, one being a favorite son if desired, as was stated in Article II, Section 1, Clause 3. Amendment 12 also states that in case of a tie for president, the House of Representatives will vote to break the tie, and in the case of a vice presidential tie, the Senate will vote to break that tie. There is more to this amendment, but for the purpose of our limited overview of this document, it will be passed over.

The separate ballots of president and vice president will gradually give way, as political parties begin to grow and exert their power and influence.

CHAPTER 20

THE POST CIVIL WAR AMENDMENTS
AMENDMENTS 13, 14 and 15

AMENDMENT 13 THE ABOLITION OF SLAVERY (1865)

This amendment simply makes a statement that no involuntary servitude will exist in the United States and its possessions except as punishment for a crime. This amendment recognizes the fact that if a person is duly convicted of a crime, labor can exist as a punishment. Thus we have had the expressions: "Work gangs," "chain gangs" and "hard labor." There has to be a delicate balance however, between this clause justifying labor as punishment for a crime and Amendment 8 of the Bill of Rights which safeguards against cruel and unusual punishment.

Clause 2 of this amendment simply states that Congress can make the laws necessary to enforce this amendment.

After the twelfth amendment became part of the Constitution, the United States went through sixty-one years uninterrupted until another amendment appeared on the scene. As was mentioned before, this was a lifetime to many of the citizens living in the 19th Century. Within a span of just five years, three amendments made their grand appearance.

An observation of the date of the first of these (1865 - same year as the end of the Civil War) and the fact that these amendments deal with the abolition of slavery, rights of citizens and voting rights to all colors and creeds and previous servitude, will lead you to the assumption that these three amendments superceded and were the direct result of the North winning the Civil War.

Today, when the demand for jobs far exceed the supply, it is difficult to understand a problem that existed at the beginning of colonial times - a shortage of farm workers. The shortage of labor may allow for an understanding of the course of action that these farmers took. This course of action that they pursued precipitated an important direction that the United States followed in its early development.

In the beginning the first Virginia Colony, known as Jamestown, was actually going down as failure. It seemed that the investors in England who formed into a company for the purpose of making profit, was about to realize that their business venture was faltering.

At first the Jamestown colonists were set up in a type of communal society. They were to work common fields and store their harvest in a communal storehouse. It was realized very early that this type of pre-communistic configuration was not too reliable. The settlers lacked the incentives that are usually associated with private ownership of farms. Because of the failure of this communal economy, the private enterprise system came about. This helped a little, but the shareholders were still singing the blues over profits not being made. Something started to change in Europe that began to change the lives of the Virginia settlement and the entire world.

European explorers were exposed to a new experience when they first started to come in contact with the native Americans. These explorers were introduced to tobacco. During the course of the early years, tobacco would be taken back to Europe and England and would become a fad, like so many other fads that have always been prevalent in man's existence. This fad, unlike the others, however, would not fade away but would become deeply ingrained, flourish and grow stronger in humans throughout the centuries. At first this new product would be smoked in pipes, rolled into cigars or chewed. The cigarette would come later - so would the hacking, wheezing, shortness of breath, yellowed fingers, burnt weeds mouth odor and general pollution.

The Virginia Colony began to flourish when they started to raise tobacco. Tobacco became so important and valuable, that people began to grow it, like flowers, around the perimeter of their houses and everywhere else they could grow it. Tobacco was carried and counted out as a person would count out money to make a purchase. Consequently, the rationale prevailed that, with all this land, the more tobacco that a person could grow, the more money he could make.

A limit existed to this kind of reasoning, however. Although land was abundant, there was only so much of it that a farmer with his sons could farm. This was before the industrial revolution made its mark upon agricultural technology. Fortunate was the farmer who had many sons, for they were a very good source of labor.

Men came from the Old World not to work for someone else. If they were to risk life and limb to get to this New World, it would be to share in the dream of becoming a land owner and not a field hand. The land owners in England were of the nobility class and demanded great respect from English citizens. An opportunity existed in the New World for a person of lowly birth, to come to these shores to become a landowner also. This is what the American dream was all about.

Where could a farmer from Virginia turn for field laborers that he so desperately needed? The Indians did not provide a good source of labor - working them was tried without success. There was an endless supply, however, of labor in the hobbles of London but that was 3000 miles away. Many men and women in England would gladly come to this new world and share in this tremendous opportunity but most would never be able to accumulate the amount of money needed for passage across the Atlantic Ocean.

Farmers worked through agents for the purpose of getting laborers for their farms. The farmer would pay for the passage of a person to come over to work for him. The worker had to sign a contract - an indenture - stating that he would work for the farmer for seven years without pay, to receive only the advantage of room and board which was to be provided by that farmer. After seven years, the farmer was to help the servant to establish himself. Because of the indenture that they signed, these workers were known as indentured servants. Not many stayed on as work hands with their former masters when their contracts expired - land was too available and these ex servants wanted to share in the American dream.

Successful farmers also subscribed to an agency that advertised for women to come to the new world to become wives to these women-less farmers. What men would look for in women today would probably be different from the expectations that the farmers had of females back in colonial times. They needed mates that would share in the backbreaking work of farm life and the more muscles the better. Very fortunate would be the farmer that obtained a wife that could produce for him, many sons. Hopefully, the mail-order bride would be more than just a bearer of children - companionship was desperately needed in that very solitary existence.

The first boat-load of African slaves arrived in Virginia around 1619. Here was a quick way to solve the growing labor problem. At first the same policy existed for the African as did the indentured servant. He would be set free after seven years of labor. It wasn't long after, that it was decided not to give the African his freedom.

As years went by, slavery flourished somewhat and then began to show signs of dying out in the United States. By the time of the writing of the Constitution, many felt that it would die a natural death due to the fact that it was not economically feasible to maintain a slave. Some feel this was the reason for the fact that slavery was not any bigger an issue than what it was during the Constitutional Convention.

With the invention of Eli Whitney's cotton gin, slavery would rise to great heights in the South. The market for cotton was available but there was a bottleneck in the farmer's production of cotton. It was very difficult to get the seeds out of the cotton and therefore a concern for the limited planting of cotton existed. With the cotton gin, the seeds could be removed more rapidly then could ever be imagined and the plantation owners became determined to produce as much cotton to feed the hungry textile mills of England and the United States as possible. To produce all this cotton, labor was needed and slavery was the most convenient answer to their labor problem.

The population of slaves, instead of declining as it had been doing, now began to rise to great heights and the institution of slavery began to imbed itself so deeply in the South that the entire economy became dependent on that institution.

Several years before the Civil War, the Supreme Court in the *Dred Scott Decision,* established the fact that slaves had no right to use the courts, and that a slave was a man's property, as was his clothes, horse and carriage. It further stated that the Constitution guaranteed that a man's property should be protected and that protection gave him the right to take his property anywhere in the United States. This decision broke down the boundary line between Slave and Free States which was shakily helping to hold the Union together. Along with several more incidents that occurred in the 1850's, this decision helped to ultimately bring about the War between the States. It took a Civil War, the complete destruction and rebuilding of the South in order for the United States to rid itself of this blight of slavery.

While this war was in progress, Lincoln issued forth his very famous Emancipation Proclamation which stated that on January 1863, all slaves in those states that are in rebellion against the United States would be freed. He made sure to say those states "in rebellion" because there were several slave states that remained neutral in this war. Lincoln had no control whatsoever over those Confederate states and not one slave was set free as a result of this proclamation while the war raged on. It was a very important document, however, and a stroke of genius on the part of the president. This document changed the reason for the war and justified it in the eyes of the White Northerners, Blacks, and citizens of foreign nations. I explained previously the need for becoming the "good guy" in an armed conflict.

No longer was this a war on the part of one section of a nation to bring back, by force, another section of that nation because they no longer wanted to belong. This war became a noble crusade to free slaves. The North became the good guys in this conflict thanks to Lincoln's Emancipation Proclamation.

The good guy image paid off. England, whose interest in this war was with the South because of the need for the cotton that was being supplied to English mills, wanted to aid the South and trade cotton for arms. The South was relying on this when they entered the war. However, the people of England put pressure on their government so as not to be a party to aiding that section of the country which was fighting to maintain the institution of slavery.

The North won the war, the South was destroyed economically, culturally and every way possible, and every effort was made to reconstruct it. It was with this background of events that the 13th Amendment was brought about.

The institution of slavery was laid to rest in the South as a result of the Emancipation Proclamation but the North had to win the war first in order for it to be put into effect. This proclamation didn't, however, free those slaves in the neutral border states. The 13th Amendment would complete the job.

CHAPTER 21

AMENDMENT 14 and 15

AMENDMENT 14 THE RIGHTS OF THE PEOPLE (1868)

This is one of the longest amendments of the twenty-six. It is similar to Article VI of the original Constitution in that it is a "catch all" for several unrelated sections. It is imperative therefore, that each section of this amendment be mentioned separately.

Section 1. A definition of what constitutes a citizen of the United States is set down in this section:

All persons born or naturalized in the United States and subject to the jurisdiction thereof, are citizens of the United States and of the state wherein they reside.

The qualification for citizen was never explained in this document before. It emphatically stresses that no state shall abridge these privileges of citizenship as set forth in this section.

The next clause of the section is important because as was already mentioned, a Supreme Court decision was made on the basis of the due process of law clause, which opened up direct line from this Federal Document to the states. It orders that the privileges set forth in our Federal Constitution are to be practiced by all state governments:

No state shall make or enforce any law which shall abridge the privileges or immunities of citizens of the United States; nor shall any state deprive any person of life, liberty, or property, without due process of law; nor deny to any person within its jurisdiction the equal protection of the laws.

Amendment Fourteen was foremost in placing the ex slave into the mainstream of American life. It is sad that this amendment, along with Amendment 18, has been the most abused and least obeyed in our Constitution. The South was simply not going to obey it and through the years openly and publicly disobeyed it through governmental maneuvering, trickery and intimidation. The North paid lip service to the amendment and was more subtle in its disregard.

In 1896 a milestone was reached in the *Plessy vs Ferguson* Supreme Court decision which stated that segregation was constitutionally legal so long as Blacks had things equal to the Whites. The segregation of the races lasted until the Supreme Court declared that segregation was not constitutionally just, in *Brown vs Board of Education of Topeka (1954)*. That decision plus the Civil Rights movements of the 1960's did away with legal segregation and integration became the order of the day. At that time Blacks began to demand and fight for those rights that were given to them in the 14th and 15th Amendments. Integration did not come easy - viewing the confrontations of the 60's on old TV news clips will ascertain those unsettled times.

It was stated in Chapter 5 that the Three-fifths Compromise allowed the South to count three-fifths of their slaves for the purpose of representation and taxation. Section 2 of Amendment 14 changes that clause as it was written in Article I. The total number of citizens within the state will now determine the representatives that states will have. It also states that if duly qualified persons are not allowed to vote, the Federal Government will punish that state by taking away some representatives. This clause has never been enforced although Blacks were denied their voting rights in many states.

Some believe that Section 3 of Amendment 14 was an exercise in punishment by those who felt that the South deserved to be punished. It disenfranchised (took the voting privilege away) and forbade from holding any office those Southerners who where officials in the United States government and when the conflict started, resigned their posts and joined the Confederacy to rebel against the United States Government.

Section 4 declared that the United States government will pay the debts incurred as a result of the Civil War. However it forbade the repaying of specific debts to those who had invested or loaned money to the South during this war.

Section 5 simply states that Congress has the right to pass laws to carry out this amendment.

AMENDMENT 15 THE RIGHT TO VOTE (1870)

This Amendment gave the ex-slave the right to vote. Section 1 says in effect that the right *to vote shall not be denied or abridged by the United States or any state on account of race, color or previous condition of servitude.*

Section 2 again simply states that Congress can pass laws necessary to carry out this amendment.

Many methods were employed in the South to keep the Negro from voting. Intimidation abounded as some whites formed into terror groups, the most infamous was the Ku Klux Klan. The poll tax came about as a method to keep Blacks from voting. Most Blacks were too poor to pay the tax necessary for voting. This helped to exclude the poor Whites also.

Blacks were intimidated or tricked into staying away from the polls in some instances. The more subtle literacy test was used also. There is nothing wrong with a literacy requirement as long as both Whites and Blacks read from the same book. There had been cases where the White man, upon registering to vote had to read and explain a passage from a very elementary reader, whereas the Black was given a passage from Shakespeare and asked to explain it. In some cases passages from the Constitution had to be read and interpreted by both Black and White thus keeping a lot of people from voting.

Grandfather clauses were incorporated into Southern law books which stated that if your grandfather voted in certain election years you were exempt from taking the literacy test. The grandfathers of the Whites were the only ones to have voted and this excluded Blacks from these exemptions.

A story which gives testimony to the inequality of voting in the South, circulated for years about the White man who went to register and was asked to read from a very simple first grade primer. An old Black man came in to register and was given a Chinese newspaper to read. He looked at the newspaper written in Chinese and said, "Now I don't know what that there headline says, but down here in the corner, in small print, it says that us Colored folk ain't going to vote again in this election this year."

CHAPTER 22

AMENDMENT 16, 17 and 18

AMENDMENT 16 INCOME TAX (1913)

The Congress shall have power to lay and collect taxes on income, from whatever source derived without apportionment among the several states, and without regard to any census or enumeration.

After the 15th Amendment was incorporated into the Constitution, forty-three years went by before Amendment 16 made its grand entrance. This is the one we love so much, especially around March and April of each year. This amendment authorized the Federal Government to impose an income tax on the citizens of the United States. If Article I, Section 9, Clause 4 of the Constitution was reviewed it would read as follows:

No capitation or other direct tax shall be laid, unless in proportion to the census or enumeration herein before directed to be taken.

This particular clause states that the Federal Government could not place a tax directly on its citizens. Taxation under this clause would have to take place proportionately according to the population of the state. Citizens were taxed indirectly by the Federal Government.

During the Civil War, Congress passed the first income tax law against Lincoln's wishes. Lincoln felt that higher taxes would take away the support that citizens had toward that war. Money was needed, however, so the country experienced its first income tax law. This law was abandoned after the war.

There was a very practical reason for the need of an income tax. When our country first started out under this Constitution, the Federal Government played a very minor roll in the lives of American citizens - most everything was left up to the state governments. As years went by, slowly the American people began to look toward the Federal Government for more and more services. As already mentioned, it seemed that the states were either unwilling or unable to meet the demands of the people.

As the central government began to do more and more, it became evident that more money was needed by the Federal Government to provide these many new services.

Progressive groups around the turn of the century felt that an income tax was needed, and even though their demands seemed to be too far out in left field in those days, almost everything that these groups advocated would slowly be worked into the mainstream of political life. In 1894, Congress again passed a two percent income tax on individuals and businesses, but this law was declared unconstitutional by the Supreme Court on the basis of Article I, Section 9, Clause 4.

By 1913, the Progressive movement that started out with a group of liberals that were looked upon as weird and ofttimes un-American, began to take hold - it became fashionable to be progressive. In the decade mentioned and the 1920's, the 16th, 17th, 18th and 19th Amendments would be added, after a void of 43 years. These new amendments were a tell-tale sign that great changes were taking place in American life.

AMENDMENT 17 POPULAR ELECTION OF SENATORS (1913)

Section 1 of the 17th Amendment gave the right to vote for United States Senators to the people.

Section 2. When a Senate seat becomes vacant the Governor of that state will call a special election to fill the vacancy. The state governments can empower the governors to fill those vacancies until an election can be held.

Section 3 filled an immediate need when the amendment came into effect. It simply stated that those Senators still in office who were previously picked by their state legislators, were not effected by this new amendment and could retain their seats. This section no longer applies because of the time factor.

It had been stressed several times that many of the framers of our Constitution were reluctant to have the common people participate too much in government. When the Constitution was first adapted, the people were limited to electing only their representatives. Democracy, as we know it today, grew slowly - fed by the likes of Jefferson, Jackson and Teddy Roosevelt to mention only a few. Eventually, the right to have a voice in electing presidents, fell into the hands of the people and now with the passing of the 17th Amendment the cycle was completed. Senators are now elected by popular vote.

In the past, the selecting of U.S. Senators was the job of the state legislatures. These Senators would represent the state governments in true federation style. This practice was a carry over from the Articles of Confederation and, as part of the Great Compromise when the Constitution was being put together, the small states were appeased. As time passed, the role of the Senate changed by slowly beginning to represent the people of the state. Even though the state legislatures elected senators, candidates still campaigned in order to have the people influence their state governments who actually did the selecting.

AMENDMENT 18 PROHIBITION (1919)

Section 1 *After one year from the ratification of this article the manufacture, sale, or transportation of intoxicating liquors within, the importation thereof into, or the exportation thereof from, the United States and all territory subject to the jurisdiction thereof for beverage purpose is hereby prohibited.*

Section 2 Declares that both the Federal Government and the states shall have concurrent power to enforce this amendment.

Section 3 This section simply gives the method by which the amendment would be ratified.

Amendment 18 is truly the most unique and interesting amendment in the entire Constitution. The passing of this amendment has been referred to as the "noble experiment," and we learned a lesson from this experiment about the futility of trying to legislate morality.

The abuse of alcohol is well known. Although many of us can have a few drinks and leave it alone, it is not the case with others. In today's world, we can see the horror and sadness that the abuse of alcohol has brought about. It was the same in the 19th century. When placed beside the deplorable conditions of the industrial urban centers, there were few other degrading powers with which alcohol could be compared.

As our industrial nation grew bigger, the working conditions worsened. Any kind of kindred spirit that once was present in small shops between workers and owners, began to fade into the smoke produced by the rapidly growing huge factory system. Owners intrusted their factories to impersonal managers who maintained their lucrative positions by being able to produce the most with the least amount of expense. As long as there were multitudes of jobless people gathering outside the factory gates pleading for work, the owners and managers could call the shots. Most workers did a single repetitious job all day which required very little skill, so they could be replaced easily. Skilled workers, as always, had more security. Women and children were used abundantly because they would work for much less pay.

The living conditions around the factories were also deplorable. People were squeezed together in small and very unsanitary rooms and apartments.

There was no chance for improvement, because wages were so that living conditions were sub standard. The work places were dirty, ill ventilated, poorly lighted and unsafe. If workers complained to the boss, the typical answer would be, "If the workers don't like it they can go somewhere else." Of course there was no other place to go and the workers were forced to feel fortunate that they were working.

With the working conditions the way they were, there was a tremendous need for any type of escape. Many workers found their escape in alcohol. Now few would argue that these people, who worked up to 15 hours a day, six days a week were not entitled to a little relaxation. The workers, however got paid so little that every dime that they spent on their libation took away some food, clothing or medicine from their families. Many times there were poverty stricken families; dirty, hungry and shoeless, standing outside of the pub imploring the "breadwinner" to come out and share the pay with his family. This was definitely one of many forms of alcohol abuse. So many could see the evils of alcohol that it became known as "demon rum."

Church groups, and various temperance associations began to fight against old "demon rum." The Women's Christian Temperance Union was the most famous. Some ladies took it upon themselves to fight the evils of whiskey by using a more aggressive approach. They would actually go into bars armed with clubs or hatchets and proceed to smash the bottles of whiskey on the shelves. One such women was a little old lady by the name of Carrie Nation. She put fear into the hearts of many bartenders. I remember seeing a picture of an old make shift saloon, out in the wild West, with a banner spread over the entrance declaring: "All nations welcomed, except Carrie."

By 1917 there were enough people in this country to realize that alcoholic beverages was a blight on this nation and there was enough support to pressure the Congress to work toward an amendment that would remove "Demon Rum" from the American scene. It became our 18th Amendment in 1919.

This truly was a great experiment. Had it worked just think of the good it would have done in those days. Think of the victims of alcoholic fathers who would have more food in their stomachs, shoes on their feet and fewer scars on their brains. Consider the lack of ruined lives and the absence of the despair that has always been the bedfellow of excessive alcohol abuse. In modern times, think of the graves that would not be filled because of drunken rages and drunken drivers. How many empty cells would we have in our prisons?

The reality of all these things could have come to pass - except for one minor detail. The American people did not want to stop drinking. In fact, the consumption of alcohol began to rise. Now that it was illegal, there was an effervescence of excitement in it that was never present before.

Men who knew about the distillation process, began to make the stuff in little neighborhood proportions. This home made substance took on the names of moonshine, bathtub gin, hootch, booze and many other terms of endearment. Once it became known that there was money in the manufacturing of this booze, it began to be made on an even larger scale. Americans who were knowledgeable in the distillation process were brought in from backwoods America and Brewmeisters were smuggled in from other countries to add an element of sophistication to this product. Monopolies began to be formed by these bootleggers so far as city blocks were concerned and eventually, the control of bigger parts of the city fell into the hands of the most aggressive and cunning. These bootleggers fought for the control of larger portions of the city and inevitably there were fights to control even larger sections. It was obviously a "dog eat dog," extremely ferocious, fight for control. Bootleggers like Al Capone, because of their aggressiveness, ruthlessness and cunning, would take over entire cities and with the large amount of money obtained from illegal alcohol, they were able to buy alderman, mayors, policemen, judges and even state and federal legislators.

Gang wars persisted and every now and then a bystander would be killed, but the public was apathetic over the entire affair. "So what," they would say, "these bootleggers were supplying an important commodity, they were making money and knew the risks - too bad if an innocent bystander got killed once in a while." (Innocent victims killed in the gang drug wars of today are referred to, unemotionally, as "Mushrooms" by these gang members.) This gang war killing of old, culminated in the St. Valentine's Day Massacre - where seven men were lined up against the wall and mowed down by machine guns. *The Untouchables* was a TV series and a movie that depicted these activities of the 1920's and 1930's.

The industrial revolution changed the way the game of cops and robbers were played. No longer would the scene of the highwayman, riding his horse in pursuit of the stagecoach, be observed. In the 1920's, we have an entirely different scenario. The picture is familiar to most - the Model T Ford whipping around the street corner, men hanging on the running boards with guns blazing. These were the "Roaring Twenties." How many shows have had the scene of the gangster and his Thompson sub machine gun with the large ammunition cylinder clipped underneath it? These state of the art weapons were used in World War I and many soldiers brought them home as souvenirs. The gangsters would send people around to the ex G.I.'s homes declaring that they were "gun collectors" and bought many of these guns at very handsome prices.

The stereotype gangster that is seen in films today has been directly influenced by his counterpart of 1920. The pin striped suit, the dark colored shirt and equally dark tie, and the heavy New York accent, still make up the image of the underworld character. In reality, it was the twenties and prohibition that brought the gangster out of the "underworld" and put him on the main streets of America. It was the "in thing" to be seen in nightclubs and parties with these people. Bootlegging moonshine gave the underworld the money and prestige to go into other ventures. It seemed that organized crime became as American as motherhood and apple pie.

The bootleggers were successful because they understood all too well the principle of supply and demand. Organized crime exists and flourishes because it panders to the demands of the citizens for pornography, prostitution, gambling, drugs and many other base commodities. We faithfully endorse, even the most horrendous crimes committed by these criminals, simply by subscribing to their services. As many people of Colombia declared, "We wouldn't have the drug problem in Colombia if there wasn't so much of a demand for drugs in the United States." Never has the following expression born more validity, however in a different light: "We get what we pay for."

If the reader is left hanging as to the outcome of this amendment, he should wait, with great anticipation, for a few more amendments to pass by, in order to find out what happened to it.

CHAPTER 23

AMENDMENTS 19 and 20

AMENDMENT 19 WOMEN SUFFRAGE

Section 1 *The right of citizens of the United States to vote shall not be denied or abridged by the United States or by any state on account of sex.*

Section 2. *Congress shall have power to enforce this article by appropriate legislation.*

When I made my students aware of the fact that the first slaves were introduced into the English colonies, I informed them that the first shipment of mail-order women came around that same time also, and for the sake of provoking a lively response in the classroom, I facetiously made a sexist remark that there seemed to be some significance to that coincidence. This was all in fun and resulted in some very interesting remarks and conclusions, which is a good tool in learning. However, there seemed to be some underlying relevance to this observation.

Women, as did slaves, endured a second class type of status in the world and it did influence the role that they played in America. Like every other issue in and on the American scene, those who had the advantages of the status quo cared little for, or violently opposed any hint of change. Those who were adversely affected by the status quo, endeavored in different degrees and methods to bring about its demise.

Thus it was with the status of women. Sometimes the biggest opponents of any change in the status of women were women themselves who were completely happy with the way things were.

Women throughout history seemed to be regarded somewhat as second class citizens. The classic picture that stays in my mind is the man on the donkey and the women walking a few respectful steps behind carrying the bundles. Other than a few matriarchal societies, where women dominated, this classic picture was world wide.

In Western civilization the laws of primogenitor stated that the estate of the father would be given to the eldest son. The eldest daughter played no part in this except in the unfortunate situation where the father had no sons in which to pass along his estate. Only then did the eldest daughter get the inheritance. Upon the marriage of that daughter the property would pass along to her husband.

Women were considered mentally incapable of grasping the concepts that were considered of manly nature. It was a popular belief that a conversation over politics would absolutely blow a woman's mind. After a meal in days past, the men would gather in the living room, light up their cigars and pipes and talk politics while the women retired to the kitchen or other designated area to discuss womanly concerns such as sewing, cooking and bearing children. This was the order of our society and most women, sometimes reluctantly, accepted it as the way things were.

Heaven help the women who tried to do damage to this pattern of life. Those women who tried to enter the world of men were severely criticized and became social pariahs to both men and women. Some women severely resented other women who would dare rock the boat in which they had choice seats. Men protested because they resented any type of female invasion into their masculine domain.

Some historians declare that the uniqueness that was developed in the American character was shaped by the American frontier. Early colonists brought their culture and institutions with them. As men went west - the "West" was in different places at different times in American History - patterns of culture were changed by this vigorous environment and these new western ideas began to filter back to the eastern towns and cities. At the beginning of our history, the eastern seaboard was a mirror that reflected European society, such as the attention paid to customs and institutions. The wealthy, especially in the South, up to the Civil War, paid homage to English culture by sending their children to schools in England. These wealthy plantation owners, the aristocracy of the South - land barons as they sometimes viewed themselves, at times felt more kinship to the way of life of Great Britain then they did toward their brothers to the North and West. Their houses were decorated with English furniture and some of their clothing were English made. These English products were obtained by trading a large portion of Southern cotton for English goods. New England had its share of aristocrats also, however, they were somewhat different because of their industrially influenced society.

As people moved out West onto the frontier, the conditions and situations that prevailed there changed their philosophy drastically. The pedigree of a person's lineage was less important then how well the individual could hold up in a gunfight with Indians. A person was judged on his own merits instead of how noble of birth he was.

Our first Western president, Andrew Jackson seemed to be a leper to the "proper" Easterner. He was ridiculed for his uncouth manner. His critics were unmerciful in their attack upon Rachel, his wife. She was previously married and, unknown to her at the time of her marriage to Jackson, her divorce was not technically completed. Jackson's opponents labeled them adulterers. He fought several duels as a reaction to remarks made about Rachel. The story goes that Rachel smoked a pipe, as many frontier women did at the time and she did not possess the "qualities" of the Eastern woman. Jackson could also see through the obsequious overtures of the opportunists that surrounded him and he made many enemies because he did not play the game by Eastern rules. In spite of all this he was an excellent president.

Many forerunning ideas about women's rights grew seed in the West. There was always a shortage of this fair sex on the frontier and a tremendous respect for women prevailed. Farming was very hard on the frontier and the women shared in this hardship, so much so that the reports were that the frontier took a deadly toll on these "fair creatures." They were haggard and worn out at age thirty. I recall a description of a day in the life of a frontier woman. It tells of her getting up earlier than the rest of the family so that she could have breakfast ready for them. It went on to describe the grueling, backbreaking chores that she had during the day and how she stopped her work when her time was right to give birth to her baby.

The worth of a woman was taken at face value on the frontier - just as the worth of a man. It is evident as women began to break out of their socially confining cocoons and started to get the right to vote and to become professionals, that it was the Western States where many of these practices were first noted.

When the men first came West without women, especially to the gold fields of California, the descriptions written about them, and old photographs that were taken, depicted them as unwashed, disheveled, drunken and slovenly. This remained true until women began to inhabit the West and change the males' erring ways.

Some say that the six shooter tamed the West, some say that it was Mr. Glidden's barbed wire. I have heard it said that it was the woman who tamed the West. She wanted the schools, the churches and the good influences for her children. She turned the heads of the male animal and brought out the best in him.

The Eastern states played an enormous part in women liberation also. The Women's Suffragette movement began to take hold, much to the chagrin of the males and many females, I might add. At times they became obnoxious to the establishment of the late 19th century. These women, some clad in Ms. Bloomer's newly designed undergarments, paraded in the city streets while the bystanders made disparaging remarks such as: "Why aren't you home taking care of your husband and children as God ordained that you should?" Many women, who did not desire change, stood on the sideline chiding them and imploring them to stop this nonsense and go home. Some women sneaked into male dominated assemblies and political meetings and they really made pests of themselves - disrupting the procedures and infuriating the males assembled there.

These women were making a statement that they were not going to be the same anymore, and as in every movement in history, this statement started out slowly and quietly and grew to influence change in our way of life. As the TV commercial once said: "You've come a long way, Baby!"

World War I proved the women's worth to the world. These so called "delicate creatures" became factory workers - taking over the physically difficult jobs once dominated by men. There was now a place for women in the armed service auxiliary and many became ambulance drivers and nurses close to the front lines. Men, whether they liked it or not, would have to do some serious rethinking so far as the women's place in the world was concerned.

To accompany, as part of and result of, all this change - was the Women's Suffrage Amendment of 1920. Some states had already allowed women the right to vote (suffrage) and it should be noticed, women's right to vote was evident in some of the Western states. This amendment ordered those states, that as yet did not incorporate women suffrage, to do so.

As depicted in many films, the "Roaring Twenties" was a time when all the efforts of women preceding that time culminated to a point where there was an outward physical change in the, appearance, activity, morality, and general attitude of the "fairer sex." The cumbersome long dresses were discarded. This freed women to participate in more physical and sport related activity. All the niceties of "feminine manners" became relaxed to the point of shocking the more conservative population right out of their spats. "Proper women" began to smoke, go to speak-easies (where illegal booze was consumed) and drive automobiles. This was the time of the short skirts, the short hair, long strings of beads and the "Charleston." To put it more crudely, the era of the "Flapper" was upon us.

Women are still at the task of equalizing the sexes. Discrimination still abounds in our society and through the effort of women, I'm sure that will change in time. I have related to my female students over the years that sometimes in order for women to become equal with men they would have to compromise the higher levels that they were at - especially so far as conduct, ethics and morality were concerned. This is certainly something that should be considered. I can remember a time, not long ago, when certain profane vocabulary was not used in the presences of those women considered to be "ladies." Lately, these "choice" words are thrown around practically everywhere, by both genders, with reckless abandon.

AMENDMENT 20 TERMS OF PRESIDENTS AND SESSIONS OF CONGRESS

THE LAME DUCK AMENDMENT

This amendment wins the prize for having the most sections of all the amendments. However Section five and six served purposes for implementing dates of effectiveness and methods of ratification, and no longer apply.

Section 1 This section moved up the date that presidents and vice presidents take office to January 20 and Senators and Representatives to January 3. Before this amendment, duly elected people to these four positions took office on March 4 and there was good reason.

Elections were held in the early part of November and those who were elected needed a longer period of time before rapid communications and transportation developed to what they are today.

It took a long time for the results of the balloting to come in and to be tallied. When the candidate learned that he won, he had to get his affairs in order so that he could begin his long journey to the capital. The time needed in the past is not needed today. In modern times it is not necessary for these newly elected officials to wait such a long time until the date for taking office arrives.

Section 2 This section reaffirms that the Congress shall meet at least once a year. This also was mentioned way back in Article 1, Section 4, Clause 2. Once they met they can make plans to meet again and again. It reiterates what was mentioned in Section 1 of this amendment, that the first meeting will be January 3. It continues to say that this date will be used unless another day is appointed by law.

Congressmen, when duly elected in November had to wait until March to take office, the rub was that the session of the legislature had already begun so the electee had to wait one complete year in order to take his office.

This is where the nickname "Lameduck Amendment" came into the picture. Those Senators and House Members who were defeated were made to stay in office one complete year before they were relieved of their duties. It was explained in a previous chapter and is quite obvious, that what makes representation work is the pressure that the office holder is under from his constituents to satisfy them. If they are satisfied they will reelection him. Imagine the attitude that would prevail in the mind of the loser? "The folks back home have rejected me and elected another. I have one full year of the job left and I'll do as little as possible for them." How many reader, at one time or other in his life had not had that attitude toward some unpleasant circumstance? The disappointed official, possibly would sit around, like a "lamé duck" not doing what he was elected to do.

Section 3 If the president elect should die between the time of his election and his going into office, the vice president becomes the president. If a president should not have been chosen or if the president elect should not have qualified, then the vice president will take over until a president shall have qualified. If both the president and vice president shall not have qualified, then the Congress shall pick someone to act as president until such time as either one shall have qualified.

I will not go too deeply into this explanation except to say that the need to cover all the contingency bases was evident in this section. The same could be said about the next section.

Section 4 If a presidential candidate should die when the House is under prescribed constitutional orders to decide a president, the House will choose a person to be president and the Senate shall do the same with a vice president.

As already mentioned, Section 5 and 6 accomplished one task and are no longer in effect.

The next amendment is the most unique of all the Amendments in this document.

CHAPTER 24 AMENDMENTS 21 and 22

AMENDMENT 21 PROHIBITION REPEALED (1933)

Let's face it, as noble as the 18th Amendment was, it was a complete failure. The good that it might have achieved is left only to speculation. Under this amendment, drinking had become the thing to do, gangsters were getting rich and some people died from gang wars and badly concocted hootch. We learned a lesson from this 18th Amendment; the government cannot legislate morality.

One of the campaign promises of Franklin Delano Roosevelt was that he would push for the repeal of the Prohibition Amendment, if he were elected the President of the United States. He was elected in 1932, took office in 1933 and the 21st Amendment came into existence that same year.

The newsreels of that time showed hordes of people packing the bars waiting for that hour when Prohibition would be officially ended and the 21st Amendment put into effect. The taps began to flow and the glasses were filled with the foamy substance that is known as beer.

This 21st Amendment is very unique in that it is the only amendment in the Constitution that was brought about for the sole purpose of doing away with another amendment.

Section 1 *The eighteenth article of amendment to the Constitution of the United States is hereby repealed.*

Section 2 *The transportation or importation into any state, territory, or possession of the United States for delivery or use therein of intoxicating liquors, in violation of the laws thereof, is hereby prohibited.*

Section 3 Tells how the amendment will be ratified. This is the only time that an amendment was ratified by state conventions instead of state legislatures. Article V stated options for the ratification of an amendment.

The rationale behind the endeavor to repeal Prohibition was the realization that people would not stop drinking and as long as they would not stop, why put the money into the hands of the bootleggers. Why not legalize it, thus having a better, safer product that the government could control and let the people indirectly benefit by imposing a tax on its sales. There is a current school of thought on the part of some Americans about legalizing drugs, which uses the same line of reasoning.

The 21 Amendment did not force the states to begin making alcoholic beverages available. It gave the states the option as to whether or not to permit this beverage within its territories. Some states in turn allowed their counties to decide that option. The situation that prevailed in the United States was the fact that we had dry states, and dry counties within states. No alcoholic beverages were allowed. This "dry" situation was evident during the thirties, forties, fifties and up to the present if there are still isolated counties in some states that fall into that category. (There may be a few of which I am not aware.)

This "dry state" or "dry county" situation really didn't stop people from drinking. Their availability problem was solved by buying "White Lightning" or going to the nearest "wet" county for their beverages. As states and counties fought among themselves to go "wet" or remain "dry" it seemed that the church people, the ministers and the bootleggers aligned themselves on the same side to keep the country "dry." Talk about strange bedfellows.

Many films have been produced based on the idea that this illegally produced moonshine or "white lightning" brought about a very lucrative situation for the bootleggers. Men modified their automobiles for hiding this commodity (in false gas tanks, etc.) and insuring that these autos were such that they could outrun any vehicle that the police and "revenue men" could put on the road. The bootleggers took pride in their automobiles and sometimes raced them with others in the same line of work. I have heard it said that it was through this effort that "stock car" auto racing came about in the South. It was in the South that more "dry" states and counties prevailed.

I can still remember traveling the East Coast Champion - the railroad between Florida and all coastal points North. Those in the club car, sipping on their libations, were notified that they were about to enter "so and so" county and because it was dry, drinks would not be sold for the minutes that it took to get through that particular county.

Some states opened up the retail of alcohol to many reliable stores but others controlled this retail through state liquor stores as did the state of Pennsylvania to mention one.

Today, as in the 19th Century, there is a growing awareness that the excessive use of alcoholic beverages is not a good thing. There exists broken homes, scared and scarred children, some poverty, and graves filled with innocent people run down by alcohol induced stupefied drivers. The problem of alcohol, most of the time, is overshadowed by the drug problem, but it does not make it any less devastating. When used excessively, it is still the "demon rum" of the last century.

Good signs are seen, however in the way alcohol consumption is beginning to be handled by the public and through the beer companies. The TV viewer is beginning to see the virtue in not driving while drinking. The beer commercials themselves are being presented as it not being an "in" thing to drink and drive. It is still very small in proportion but when one realizes the tremendous influence that television has on public opinion, it is a good sign. Judges and state legislation are becoming short of patience with the alcoholic driver abuser.

Eighteen years will go by until the next amendment.

AMENDMENT 22 TERMS OF PRESIDENTS (1951)

Section 1 *No person shall be elected to the office of President more then twice, and no person who has held the office of President, or acted as President, for more than two years of a term to which some other person was elected shall be elected to the office of President more than once.*

This section goes on to explain that this amendment will not apply to anyone holding the office of President at the time that this amendment was proposed. It did not apply to Harry S. Truman.

Section 2 This section tells how the amendment will be adopted.

The way the amendment is worded, there is a possibility that a person can be a president for one day less then ten years. If a vice president takes over one day less than the second year of the original president's term, it is considered the vice president's term and he is entitled to only one more term. If a vice president becomes president one day over the original presidents second year, that would be considered the original president's term of office and the vice president is entitled to two more terms of office.

The original Constitution simply states that a term of office of President is four years. It says nothing about how many terms a person shall have as president. It is possible that the framers felt that a man could be president, term after term after term, if he was doing a good job in that office.

George Washington served one term, was reelected again and even though he had dropped somewhat in popularity by the end of his eight years, he probably would have been elected for a third term had he run. Some historians feel that public service was getting George down and that he dreamed of the time when he could retire from serving his country and go back to his farm at Mount Vernon and live the rest of his life as a country squire. He probably deserved to take it easy.

When he was approached with the idea that he should run again, he refused, saying two terms were enough for a president. In a sense, Washington had established a precedent. John Adams, our next president, didn't have a chance to run twice, and Jefferson our third chief executive did not consider an attempt at a third term.

Custom and precedents entrench themselves more deeply as time goes on, and it becomes more difficult for them to be broken. Throughout the 19th century, no one deviated from this two term path. The idea of breaking this precedent was toyed with by a few, but the slow development of the two term idea prevailed and it was decided not to try.

With Franklin Delano Roosevelt, it was a different story. In FDR we had a very capable leader during some of the roughest times in our history. He came into office during the depression years of the early 1930's and some will admit, that through his efforts, we began to pull ourselves out of this state of affairs somewhat. In 1936 he was elected again by many Americans that were now looking upon him as the only man to go with in those trying times. In 1940, during the gathering storms of World War II, he decided to break this long standing precedent established by George Washington and run for a third term.

I was a young person at the time but I can still remember the conversations between my father and others. Some would say, "He cannot do that, it's against the law." Others who knew a little more about the Constitution would answer, "It's not against the law, it is something that has never been done before." The answer from the first person would be: "Well, it just isn't done." The third term situation was the talk of the times.

Roosevelt did it - he ran for the third term, breaking all precedents and was elected for president again. Many people had so much confidence in FDR over how well he had handled things up to that time, they felt that "changing horses in the middle of the stream" was not prudent. During those dreadfully fearful pre World War II times, people wanted someone in whom they had complete confidence as their president.

The war started and raged on during the early 1940's and when 1944 approached, the question of electing a president was upon us once again. The same type of reasoning dominated the political scene - not wanting to "change horses" made sense. Why get a new man in the oval office? FDR is in charge of things and knows what is happening and is doing a good job. We are winning the war aren't we?

FDR must have been thinking along the same line because, lo and behold, he ran again and was elected for the fourth term. He never finished this term. He died from a stroke and Harry S. Truman took over. Some Americans, especially Republicans, felt that if FDR had not died, he probably would have run for a fifth term.

There were no two ways about FDR. People either loved him or hated him because of the liberal changes that were brought forth under his administration. Magazines and newspapers had pictures showing the sorrow that accompanied his passing, while others were relieved by his death.

I can remember hearing of his death on the radio and was shocked. I was about fourteen at the time and I knew no other president. I had to tell someone. I was asked to go to the shoe repairmen to retrieve a pair of shoes for someone in the family. When I arrived at the shop I asked the proprietor if he know what had happened. The shoe repairman replied, "Yes, the dictator is dead."

After this precedent breaking ordeal, Americans began to feel that maybe this was not a good thing. Not only did FDR break a long standing precedent, but in doing what he did, he probably established another and the door was now opened for presidents to run again and again. Many did not like the idea of a president staying in office indefinitely. There was a desire to go back to the two terms per president situation before FDR. As a result we have the twenty-second Amendment.

There were ten uninterrupted years between the twenty-second and the twenty-third Amendments.

CHAPTER 25

AMENDMENTS 23, 24, 25, and 26

AMENDMENT 23 WASHINGTON, DC GETS THE RIGHT TO VOTE (1961)

Section 1 Makes it lawful for the residents of the District of Columbia to vote in presidential elections. It says that Washington, D.C. will get the same amount of electoral votes as though it were a state but no more than the least populated state. This measures out to three electoral votes.

Section 2 Empowers Congress to make such laws that are needed to carry out this amendment.

The right to vote came from the state in which a person lived. The Constitution mentions the fact that the qualification for voting in federal elections must be the same as the requirement that a state places on voting in its own elections. Remember, it was the states that came to the Constitutional Convention with all the power and what they did not give to the federal government they kept for themselves.

The Constitution gave no provision for voting in the capital city because at the time of the framing of this document, a capital city was just the dream of a few. When the city became a reality and as people moved to this city to establish residence, they lost their voting right because this city was not a part of a state from which that right could be obtained.

For decades, many inhabitants within this city circumvented the situation by holding on to their residency from other states. During election time they could go back to Virginia, or Maryland, or where ever, to cast their ballots.

There seemed to be national opposition to allowing the residents of Washington, DC to vote. Some felt that many Washingtonians were connected with the federal government and their voting would be on the basis of selfish motivation rather than a valid determination to vote for the best person for the office.

Three years passed by before the next amendment was added.

AMENDMENT 24 NO MORE POLL TAX IN NATIONAL ELECTIONS. (1964)

Section 1 No more paying of poll taxes in order to vote for presidents, vice presidents, Senators and House members.

Section 2 Congress can pass the necessary laws to carry out this amendment.

When the 15th Amendment was discussed, it was mentioned that the South tried many methods to keep the ex slaves from voting. One subtle method was the poll tax. This was a tax that had to be paid at the voting booth before a ballot was given to vote. So much poverty existed among the Blacks in those states that the small amount necessary for the privilege of voting could not be paid. Bread was more important than a ballot. Of course, this tax kept many poor whites from voting also. It also excluded those who had the money but placed paying good money to vote very low on their list of priorities.

This amendment was to ban the poll tax in federal elections only. In 1966 the Supreme Court declared the use of the poll tax in state elections to be unconstitutional also.

Three years go by until the twenty-fifth amendment appeared. It seems that the amendments began to come in steadily in the 20th century.

AMENDMENT 25 SUCCESSION OF A PRESIDENT (1967)

Section 1 This section reiterates what was stated in Article II of the Constitution - that in case of the death or resignation of a president, the vice president takes over.

Section 2 This section says that in case there is a vacancy in the office of the vice presidency, the president shall nominate a vice president upon the approval of both Houses of Congress.

Vice president Spiro Agnew resigned in 1973 because of the shadow that darkened his reputation, of alleged wrongdoing in contractual kickbacks that he received when he was a governor. President Richard Nixon appointed Gerald Ford to the vice president spot. When Nixon resigned the presidency, a year later, Ford became the President and appointed Nelson Rockefeller to the post of vice president.

Here is the answer to a very good trivia question. What President of the United States was put into that office without undergoing the normal process of election?

Section 3 The president can submit in writing to the Speaker of the House and the President pro tem of the Senate, a declaration that he is unable to carry out his duties and the vice president will become acting president until such time as the president can resubmit a declaration that he can resume his duties.

The proper order of submission of this declaration in the Senate would be to the President of the Senate, who is the Vice President of the United States. It seemed to be more prudent to submit the declaration to the President Pro Tem, thus circumventing the Vice President, who would be personally effected the most by this presidential decision.

Chapter 7 told of the stroke that had befallen Woodrow Wilson as he toured the country to try to gain support for the League of Nations. The Constitution mentioned nothing definite about such a situation and the vice president at the time did not take it on his own to act. As a result, Wilson laid around helplessly and was not able to carry out his duties. Fortunately, there wasn't too much time left on his term of office.

Eisenhower had a heart attack while in office and because he was still in sound mind, instructed then Vice President Nixon to mind the store until he fully recovered. This is a good practice, until you get into a situation where the president would lack the mental capacity to delegate his duties to the vice president. What would happen next? There was a book and subsequent movie about a president who was losing his mind so subtlety that only a few realized it. It really made a person think about the reality of such a situation.

When Kennedy was shot, he lived for about 20 minutes with severe damage to his brain. The question arose later, "What if he had lingered in a vegetable like state? Could the succession of power have gone smoothly to the next in line? I remember once, these questions being presented on many TV news shows and newspapers as a result of this heart rendering tragedy.

Section 4 This section deals with removing the president for reasons that would render him unable to carry out his duties, when it is not on the voluntary suggestion of the president himself.

The vice president and the president's cabinet may declare the president unable to carry out his duties. If the vice president and the cabinet disagree, then it will be decided by a two-third vote of Congress as to whether or not the president can carry out his responsibilities.

As a safeguard check and balance, the involuntary removal of a president can become the responsibility of two branches of government if need be - the Executive and the Legislative Branches.

After a time the president can declare in writing that he is once again fit but he will not resume his duties if the vice president and cabinet declare that he is still unable. Of course, the vice president takes over the helm during all this.

For the sake of brevity, I did not mention the time sequence involved in the different phases between submitting and performing different tasks in this amendment.

Three and a half years go by before we come to the last of these amendments - twenty-six.

AMENDMENT 26 THE VOTING AGE (1971)

Section 1 The right of citizens of the United States, who are 18 years of age or older, to vote shall not be denied or abridged by the United States or any state on account of age.

Section 2 Congress shall have the power to enforce this article by appropriate legislation.

When we were kids, we couldn't wait to be 21 years old. At that time twenty-one was the legal age. As a teenager, it meant - not so much being able to vote - but to legally go into bars. We used to hang around the street corners and fantasize about reaching that adulthood age. I can remember some of the conversations even today. "I am going into the bar just before midnight and they will ask for my ID and tell me that I am not old enough but I'll sit there until after midnight and ask for the biggest drink they can make." I fantasized in this a little also.

I happened to turn 21 while going to school at the Naval Gun Factory in Washington D.C. The drinking age there at that time was 18 years. It seemed that I missed out on a good chunk of my fantasy.

There was discontentment over the idea that 21 was the proper age of adulthood. The argument at the foreground was; if a person was old enough at 18 to be drafted into the armed services and old enough to give his life for his country he certainly should be old enough to vote and go to bars. How could a person argue against this?

Against the backdrop of this argument and others, Amendment 26 came into being.

CHAPTER 26 CONCLUSION

In a little over two hundred years our Constitution has had only twenty-six amendments. If one considers the fact that the first ten were added as one of the first obligations of the U.S. Congress, then it can be rightfully said that in a period of only 200 years we have had sixteen individual additions. This fact adds to the prestige of the Constitution and bears witness to the good job that the framers did.

In a constantly changing world, a constitution must possess within it the capability of taking on the aspects of change. Our forefathers were aware of this as they constructed Article V to allow for change within this document.

The capability for change also came about through the process of interpretation. It was an interpretation itself that gave the Constitution that characteristic. Through the judicial process, we are constantly seeing decisions and rulings entering the picture to give this document new twists. Of course precedence and customs are a part of this picture also.

Because of these factors, we have a document that will flex with changing times. Without this flexibility, it would have been too rigid and could have possibly shattered as a result of the many changes that have taken place in the United States, especially during the 20th century.

We cannot prognosticate the changes of the future, but we can stand confident in the fact that our Constitution will be capable of meeting those changes head on - either through judicial interpretation or amendment.

The fact that we have had only sixteen individual changes could lead a person to the conclusion that we have had a pretty slow 200 years, and that need for change was not evident. This is untrue. We have had over 1000 proposals for amendments, and very few have made the grade.

Because of the difficult road that a proposed amendment has to travel in order to become a reality, the enormous number of those proposals have fallen by the wayside. This seems to be a good thing - could you imagine our Constitution with over 1000 amendments?

On one hand there are those who are so moved by the need for change, they feel the only solution to a serious problem would be an amendment. On the other hand we have those who feel that our Constitution should be interfered with as little as possible. It is a good thing that a Constitutional change involves so many people and so many institutions, otherwise the process laid out in Article V would be much over-used.

Sometimes a very unfavorable Supreme Court decision sets forth an unpopular reaction. Those adversely affected by the decision will rush to Article V to try to change the very interpretation itself. A prime example was the furor unleashed when the Court declared that the law against flag burning was unconstitutional. Needless to say the attempt at an amendment to prohibit flag burning was unsuccessful. Many who opposed the amendment were not in favor of flag burning by any means. They were opposed to violating the uncluttered appearance of the Constitution itself.

Amendment 11 was brought about by negative reaction to a Supreme Court decision which allowed a person to sue a state government in a federal court. The states, not wanting this situation, pushed for a Constitutional amendment to do away with this and give the jurisdiction to the state that was being sued.

There have been many proposed amendments that have fallen by the wayside, even in modern times. The Equal Rights Amendment that many women pushed religiously and the proposed amendment that would balance the budget. I imagine it depends upon how dedicated a person is to a certain cause, whether he is for Constitutional change or not. As was mentioned, these proposed amendments have a long arduous road to follow and one can easily lay odds on most of them to fail.

Oh, by the way, some may still be waiting for the solution to the Frankenstein dilemma found in chapter three - the fear of the monster turning against the creator. This fear prompts him to build a small monster that he would not have to fear, but would afford him little protection. The obvious answer is found in the first three articles of the Constitution. Instead of building one gigantic monster twelve feet tall, why not build three, each four feet tall. If one should turn against the creator, he has the other two to come to his aid. All three of them working in unison would bring together a power of very great significance. Now a person may respond to this by saying that all three could turn against the creator. This is true except that the likelihood of this happening is far less than having only one to turn.

This is what the framers did to protect us from the awesome power of the government that they were establishing - they divided this power into three separate channels, or branches. If one should go bad then there were two others to ride herd on the errant branch.

Never had a year gone by, in the process of explaining this to my students, that one of them would not ask the question: "What happens should all three go bad?" My answer to them was that the people themselves, from which this power is obtained, act as the final check and balance. When the people themselves get into the process of "cleaning house," things begin to happen. However, the people must be informed as to what is happening in their government in order for them to do this. The people must know enough to care, and care enough to know.

I also used the above paragraph to answer my students when they asked me the question: "Why do we need to study this stupid Social Studies?" I went on to tell them, "Someone once wrote that the citizens of a democratic nation get the kind of government that they deserve - no more or no less." Unfortunately, these "gems of wisdom" that I showered on my students through the years rolled off many of their heads, as water rolls off of a duck's back. I realize that these were young people to whom I was trying to get the message across and maturity for them was still lurking around the corner. Regretfully, there are some adults out there whose complete apathy would allow the water on their heads to do likewise. I hope their numbers are few and far between.

We need informed citizens in order to survive in a free society. We need the protesters and those who feel the urge to argue a point. However, we must look objectively at both sides of an issue before we take up our placards and signs to join in the street march. It is imperative that we have news about our nation and world that is as trustworthy as possible because of its massive and rapid availability through our newspapers and televisions. If the information that we receive is not valid, if we form our opinions on misinformation or if we blindly follow others, then we are not totally free.

It is my desire that this book would shed some light somewhere - maybe to add an iota of understanding or an ounce of appreciation for this great document that is ours - The Constitution of the United States of America.